CRAFTY * CLOWNS

DI CAMPBELL

*

A DAVID & CHARLES CRAFT BOOK

ABBREVIATIONS

These are used throughout the book.

RS — Right side
WS — Wrong side
RS tog — Right sides together
WS tog — Wrong sides together
SA — Seam allowance
CF — Centre front
CB — Centre back
DK — Double knitting

ENGLISH/AMERICAN GLOSSARY

English	American
Bias binding	Bias strip
Bradawl	Spike, stiletto
Brooch pin	Jewelry pin
Buttonhole thread	Buttonhole twist
Cocktail stick	Toothpick
Copydex adhesive	Latex adhesive/Slomans
Cotton wool	Surgical cotton
Craft stick	Wooden stick knobbed at both ends
Dolly peg	Wooden clothes pin with knob at one end
Elastic bands	Rubber bands
Fablon	Sticky-backed vinyl
Fimo	Plastic modelling material Polyform/Sculpey/Formello
Hardboard	Fibreboard
Iron-on interfacing	Non-woven fusible interface
Muslin	Cheesecloth
Pile fabric	Napped fabric
Plasticine	Re-usable modelling clay Plasteline
Polyester toy stuffing	Polyester fibrefill
Polyester wadding	Polyester batting
Sellotape	Thin sticky tape/Scotchtape
Stockinette	Cotton-knit fabric
Tack	Baste
Velvet	Silky napped fabric
Velveteen	Cotton napped fabric

British Library Cataloguing in Publication Data
Campbell, Di
   Crafty clowns. – (A David & Charles craft book)
   1. Handicrafts. Special subjects. Clowns
   I. Title
   745.592

   ISBN 0-7153-9390-1 H/B
   ISBN 0-7153-0123-3

First published 1990
Reprinted 1991
First published in paperback 1993

© Di Campbell, 1990

Typeset in Century Old Style by ABM Typographics Ltd, Hull
and printed in Portugal by Resopal
for David & Charles
Brunel House   Newton Abbot   Devon

Contents

FOREWORD

Everyone loves a clown whether it be a red-nosed Auguste or white-faced Venetian, tearful Pierrot, symbol of unrequited love, or colourful Harlequin. From the Italian Commedia dell'Arte to the travelling circus the clown represents a beloved figure in the imagination of child and adult alike. Harlequino, Scaramouche, Pagliaccio and their motley troupe have been favourite subjects for artists and composers through the centuries and up to the present day. The clowns in this book are a small sample of variations on the theme, including dolls, a quilt, a dressing-up outfit, traditional toys and some novelties. Many clown dolls produced commercially are either mawkish or downright frightening, extremes which I have tried to avoid. Fur fabric (fakefur), so popular in the realm of mass-production, is my own least favourite fabric and this has been almost completely ignored in favour of cotton, satin and velvet.

As toys and craft products in shops get more and more expensive there is a definite need for the well-made, home-produced article which gives satisfaction both to the recipient and the maker. Most of the designs in this book are easy to reproduce but some assume a certain amount of skill and knowledge in needlecraft. For guidance the items are graded with stars ☆: 3 for a complex project, 2 for a fairly easy one and 1 for work which can be tackled by a beginner. All the instructions are detailed and comprehensive with plenty of diagrams, which, when followed carefully, will give delightful results.

Use your own discretion with regard to colour choices but be aware of a few basic rules. Rather than trying to match up too many materials of one colour, on what is a relatively small area, go for contrast or harmony instead. Red is notoriously difficult in this respect. Bright primary colours and pale pastels seldom mix well so keep them in separate schemes when gathering together your materials.

When making items of craftwork to a specific subject many processes are repeated. Clowns will usually have pompons and frills, some faces are embroidered in the same way and fringes of hair are attached in a similar fashion on more than one item. To avoid repetition the instructions for these, and other, components are set out in General Notes at the beginning of the book and the reader is advised to check these first. When deciding on what to make always read through the relevant text first and the references to the General Notes.

Some of the techniques explained in this book will be of use when applied to other patterns for dolls and soft furnishings and those readers who enjoy adapting patterns and designing their own will find lots of 'jumping off points' in these pages.

Just send in the clowns!

Crafty Clowns (clockwise from top left): Soup Clowns; Stripey Doll; Pyjama Case; Toilet Bag and Soap Sachet; Judy

GENERAL NOTES

FINDING MATERIALS

Always be on the look-out for good sources of fabrics. There seems to be a decline in the small town fabric shop these days so sometimes it requires a trip to a department store in a large town to see what is available. For those craftspeople who live 'out in the sticks' there is often only one way out and that is to rely on mail order catalogues. Many of these are extremely good and offer, in one parcel as it were, all the things you may have to trek miles for. Many craft magazines carry advertisements for these companies who will send brochures and samples of their wares on request.

Shops which provide inspiration are: good stationers for papers and card, variously shaped stickers etc; DIY shops for glue, paint and off-cuts of wood; knitting shops for oddments of wool and knitting cotton (candlewick). Where only small amounts of a particular fabric are required a scarf or even a handkerchief can be cut up and wide ribbons will provide small pieces of satin in a broad choice of colours. When buying stockinette (cotton knit fabric) note the amount of stretch in the fabric. When the fabric is used double as it comes, there is usually horizontal stretch only, giving an increase, when pulled, of 1cm (½in) over a space of 2cm (¾in) When buying felt always get the best quality. Some felts come apart easily and have an unpleasant surface feel. Many materials required can be improvised; for example, a discarded vest or tee-shirt can be dyed and used as stockinette.

When buying fabric from the roll remember that some is sold by the metre and some by the yard but the widths are usually standard for the type of fabric. Dress cottons are usually 92cm (36in) or 114cm (45in) wide and woollens 150cm (60in) wide. Sheeting comes in special widths to fit single or double beds, 175cm (70in) or 225cm (90in) wide or more depending on the manufacturers. The amounts of materials required in this book are given in both metric and imperial measurements. Keep to one set only.

Keeping a 'useful box' is a good idea. Mothers of small children will know this already. Keep empty containers and glossy card packaging, cellophane and left-over ribbon and wool. Everything comes in useful eventually.

EQUIPMENT

A 'zig-zag' sewing machine is useful but not essential. It comes into its own for appliqué and for finishing off seams inside a garment, although pinking shears can be used to trim the seams instead. Some of the items in this book can be made entirely by hand but a machine is needed, if only for speed, when making larger articles. You will need an iron for pressing and for applying interfacing. Have a table in a good light for cutting out on, or clear a space on the floor for very large patterns.

Some small hand tools will be needed for making the toys: a hack saw for cutting wood and cane, a medium-sized screwdriver and a bradawl (stiletto) for making holes. Some drawing aids will be necessary for copying patterns: good-quality tracing paper, some pattern paper with 5cm (2in) squares, a ruler, soft lead pencils, a ballpoint pen. For painting and decorating: some small pots of enamel, narrow paintbrushes, cleaner such as turpentine, larger pots of paint for dipping pieces and some fine marker pens in various colours.

A sharp craft knife is useful and good scissors are an essential. Small, sharp scissors are needed for cutting felt and a pair of medium-sized cutting-out scissors for the other fabrics. Keep a separate pair for cutting paper. For setting Fimo (Polyform) you will need access to an oven.

TECHNIQUES

Pattern making

Some patterns in these pages have been reduced, keeping the proportions correct, so in order to make them life-size you will have to enlarge them by the right amount. If you are lucky enough to have access to a photographic enlarger use that. Otherwise use the squared paper method. This always sounds more difficult than it is but it is a simple technique and well worth knowing. Take some squared paper on which the lines are 5cm (2in) apart horizontally and vertically. Where pattern lines on the small grid (on the page) touch a grid line, make a cross on the same line on the large-squared paper. Count the lines across and down to find the correct position. Join all the crosses in an outline to give the full-size pattern.

Most of the patterns have pieces which are given full size and these can be traced from the outlines on the page. For reasons of space, where a pattern piece is symmetrical, only half the piece is printed. Fold your tracing paper in half and put the fold to the line indicated. Trace round the outline and mark any features, direction marks etc on the paper. Cut round the outline and open up the fold. Other pieces are traced straight off the page. Use good-quality tracing paper and a black ballpoint pen.

Transferring patterns to fabrics

There are several different ways and everyone has a favourite. One of the easiest is to scribble on the back of the pattern paper with a soft pencil and place it down on the fabric. Draw round the pattern lines with a ballpoint pen. Dressmakers' carbon paper is obtainable in light and dark ink to suit different fabrics. A useful marking device is an air soluble pen which will mark fabrics for a short time then disappear after sewing. The oldest, and still useful, method is called 'pouncing' where the pattern lines are pierced with a needle and chalk dust sprinkled through the holes onto the fabric. On pale, thin fabrics try tracing the outlines and features straight onto the cloth from the page.

To make circles, draw round kitchen items that have the right diameter, eg plates and tumblers. For small circles draw round coins, or place round stickers on the fabric, cut round and discard. This method is useful for making eyes in felt. To make large circles you will need a piece of chalk and a length of string. Tie one end of the string round the chalk. Fold the fabric to be cut into quarters and place it down with the folds lying at the left-hand side and the front edge. Measure the radius (half the diameter) of the circle to be cut. Holding the string at this distance from the chalk place it down on the folded fabric with the thumb holding the string onto the lower left-hand corner. Hold tight and, pulling on the string, swing the chalk round over the fabric to mark the curve from the vertical to the horizontal edges. Cut the folded fabric on this curve and open the full circle out. Circles of any size can be cut this way.

Cutting out

When laying pattern pieces out, take note of any special requirements. 'One-way' fabrics – satin, velvet, stockinette etc – must all lie in the same direction. To cut pairs always reverse the pattern piece on the fabric. Some fabrics, satin for instance, mark easily so if you pin down the patterns do so within the SA. Don't cut into the fabric to mark positions. Notch the pattern paper instead and mark the fabric with pencil. When several small pieces of felt have to be cut and interfaced, iron them onto the backing before cutting.

SEWING INFORMATION

Before commencing sewing, check the pattern for details. The SA allowed on most pattern pieces is 1cm (½in) but different widths of SA are used depending on type of fabric and size of piece. On a stretchy fabric like stockinette it is wise to sew round (stay stitch) each piece on the seam line to prevent excessive stretching when sewing parts together. Always pin and tack seams before sewing them especially when joining slippery fabrics which 'creep' and when joining a straight piece to a curved one as when making little boots. Pin and tack a little inside the SA to avoid marking fabrics.

When preparing to sew wadded layers together, remember that a larger SA is included as the wadding takes up the top fabric somewhat. If pieces of wadding have to be joined to cover a large area, make a butt join (edge-to-edge). Use a large needle threaded with thin knitting wool and sew from side to side of the join without raising the edges. Use large, slack stitches so there will be no ridges showing under the top fabric.

When sewing curved seams always start at the halfway point and sew down each side to avoid distortion. The best thread to use when sewing by hand is stranded embroidery thread which can be bought in an abundance of shades and can be split up into different thicknesses. When sewing satin ribbon and net it damages the fabric less than an ordinary sewing thread would.

Threading beads

When a bead forms an extremity, eg a foot, hand or head, it has to be stopped from falling off. Tying a knot in the ribbon or cord is not very reliable. The best way is to use a smaller bead called a 'stop bead' at the end and pass the ribbon back through the foot, hand or head bead. Where a thick cord or ribbon has to pass through a bead try to buy macramé beads which have a large hole, or make the existing hole in the bead larger with a round file. When a lot of strands have to be passed through one bead this can be done by threading a single loop of thin yarn through the bead, passing it over the sheaf of strings and pulling it through the bead (see Fig 1).

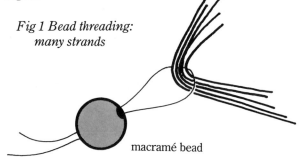

Fig 1 Bead threading: many strands

macramé bead

Bias binding (Bias strip)

This is a tape cut on the bias of the fabric. It can be bought in various widths and colours in thin cotton or satin with both edges turned in to the WS on the stitching lines (see Fig 2 for method of applying). It can be bought also with a centre fold ready for applying the tape straight to the edge to be bound. Bias-binding tape can also be used to form a placket to carry elastic or cord (see Fig 3), or to create a false hem when material is short.

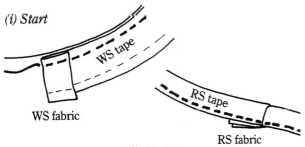

(i) Start

(ii) Finish

Fig 2 How to apply bias binding

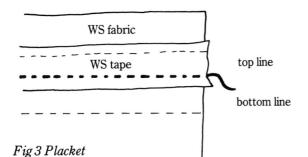

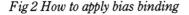

Fig 3 Placket

Elastic

When threading elastic into a placket leave a gap in the lower edge of the tape seam and use this to thread the elastic through. Thin elastic can be carried by a bodkin but wider elastic is better fastened onto a safety pin and pulled through. Another safety pin at the far end of the

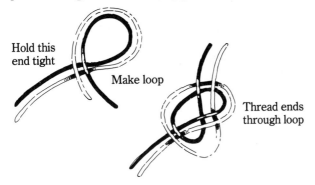

Hold this end tight

Make loop

Thread ends through loop

Fig 4 Weaver's knot. With practice this can be done between the finger and thumb of one hand

elastic will prevent it from being drawn into the placket. Tie narrow elastic together with a weaver's knot (see Fig 4) but wide elastic will have to be overlapped and stitched firmly across. When the elastic is joined, trim the ends and let it go into the placket. Close up the gap.

Cords

A drawstring fastening is the easiest closure to manage especially if the cord loops are double and pull against each other. (Fig 5). Cut two equal lengths of cord and thread each one through the hem or placket from opposite openings, round the whole of the bag top and back again to the beginning. Join each pair of ends in a weaver's knot (Fig 4).

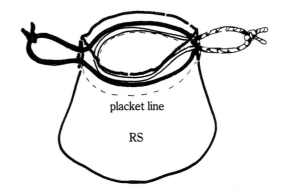

placket line

RS

Fig 5 Drawstrings

Appliqué

This is the form of decoration made by applying one layer of cloth over another. Materials of all kinds can be used but the best are the non-fraying types, eg felt. Fraying can be cut down on other fabrics by backing the pieces with interfacing. If applying the pieces by machine with a zig-zag stitch, use a close buttonhole spacing in a width wide enough to cover the edge of the appliqué piece where it meets the background. Use black thread to create a bold outline and sew down the pieces in the order shown in the instructions. A slight dab of glue will hold the pieces in place whilst sewing.

If applying pieces by hand, cut them (except felt) with a small SA, ½cm (¼in) all round. Clip the SA on

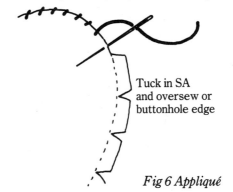

Tuck in SA and oversew or buttonhole edge

Fig 6 Appliqué

curves and press the SA to the WS of the piece. The edges can be sewn down using oversewing or buttonhole stitch round the edge (see Fig 6). An embroidery hoop is useful for holding the background fabric tight during sewing. Add embroidery details and press the finished motif under a damp cloth.

Stab stitch (Fig 7)
Starting at the back bring the needle through very close to the edge and make a tiny straight stitch through to the back again. Carry on in a line for outlining felt appliqué parts. Useful for sewing two rather thick layers together.

Stitch close to edge using stab stitch

Fig 7 Felt

EMBROIDERY STITCHES

Buttonhole stitch (Fig 8)
Machine buttonhole stitch is not really buttonhole stitch at all but simply a very close oversewing from side to side on a line, more like satin stitch (see fig 13). This is the preferred way of working appliqué but there are several versions of hand stitches which will decorate the surface of the cloth at the same time as fixing the edge, buttonhole stitch being one of these. Work from left to right creating a corded line on the very edge of the appliqué piece. Work like satin stitches but leave a loop of thread on the outside edge to be held down by the next stitch.

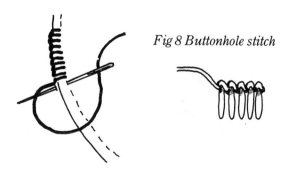

Fig 8 Buttonhole stitch

Back stitch (Fig 9)
This is a useful stitch for joining two fabric pieces together by hand or for making a line of decoration. Sew on a line from right to left. Make a small stitch to begin then insert the needle back to the beginning and out again an equal distance ahead of the stitch. The next step back covers the space behind and creates the next one ahead.

Fig 9 Back stitch

[Fig 9 illustration with points *A and *B]

Bullion stitch (Fig 10)
This is similar to a French knot (see Fig 12) but more elongated. It can be used to make a small mouth with just three stitches, two for the top lip and one for the bottom lip. Push the needle through the fabric for the length of stitch required. Wind the thread round the needle for about six times then pull the needle through the fabric and the twists. Enter the needle at the beginning of the stitch again so the twists lie in the space.

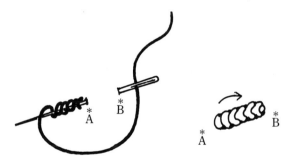

Fig 10 Bullion stitch

Daisy stitch (Fig 11)
In this stitch the thread makes a single loop which lies open on the fabric and is held down by a small stitch in the loop. Useful for making the lines round the eyes on a clown's face. Bring the needle up through the fabric and make a small loop. Hold the loop with the thumb whilst returning the needle to the place where it came in, to emerge again inside the loop the required distance of the stitch. Hold the loop down with a small stitch made over the thread of the loop, the point of the needle going back to the beginning again.

Fig 11 Daisy stitch

French knot (Fig 12)
This is the stitch for a small dot, either made singly or all over, or close together tightly for a filling-in stitch. To start bring the needle up through the fabric and make two or three twists of thread around it. Pull the needle out through the fabric and the twists, pushing the twists down onto the fabric. Insert the needle again a fraction away from where it emerged, to hold the twists in a close little bunch.

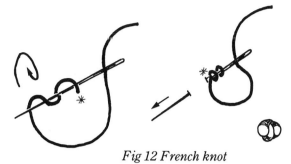

Fig 12 French knot

Satin stitch (Fig 13)
This is the best of all filling-in stitches. The area to be covered should be kept small whilst large areas should be split up into several smaller ones. Start on the outline edge at one side of the space to be filled. Carry the thread over to the point on the outline opposite. Insert the needle here to emerge again a fraction under where the stitch began. Continue in this way, matching the length of the stitch to the width of the space until the whole of the space is filled.

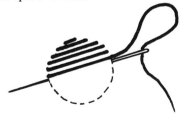

Fig 13 Satin stitch

Stem stitch (Figs 14 and 15)
This is another useful line stitch suitable for the curved line of a clown's smiling mouth. The line of stitching is worked from left to right. Start at the far end of the line with the needle coming up through the fabric on the line. Push the needle back into the fabric with the point emerging again to the left but less than half the way down the previous stitch. Each stitch is a step to the right with a shorter step back to the left. For a thin line the needle enters and emerges on the line but if a slightly thicker line is desired angle the needle slightly across the line when making the stitches. This gives a corded effect to the line (see Fig 15).

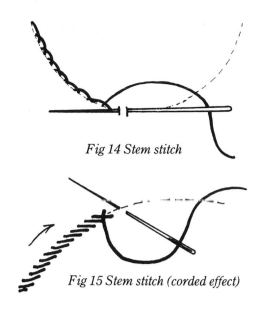

Fig 14 Stem stitch

Fig 15 Stem stitch (corded effect)

Other stitches may be equally suitable but the above-mentioned will cover the items in this book. For best effect use 'stranded cotton' embroidery thread and a crewel needle, ie a short needle with a fairly long eye. Split the thread up for smaller areas and thin fabrics but use full thickness on larger ones or where a raised surface is desired. Always use short lengths of thread and start off at the back of the work with a knotted thread. Finish off with a few tiny stitches at the back of the work. Don't be tempted to cross over to another area without cutting the thread and starting again as sometimes a white fabric face can be spoiled by black thread showing through.

If you like making dolls but dislike embroidery the features on most faces can be painted with fabric paints. These can be obtained from art and craft shops in various colours and widths of line to use direct from the tube like a pen. They are washable, won't run and can be used on most fabrics with great effect.

SPECIAL EFFECTS

Sticky bits
Throughout the book where reference is made to glue it is usually latex-based adhesive (Copydex (Slomans)). Appliqué pieces and small features can be stuck onto faces with it instead of sewing, or whilst waiting to be sewn. Ribbon bows can be stuck on instead of stitched on some items. Sequins and other decorations can be applied to surfaces with tiny dabs of it. Latex-based fabric glues are best spread thinly and, if necessary, on both parts to be joined as it is easy to squash a large blob through a thin fabric thus spoiling the surface. Latex adhesive is white to begin with but dries transparent; take care when using it though, as any

spills on clothing have to be removed with petrol. 'Super glue' may be needed to join wood, metal or ceramics but use it with extreme caution and only when nothing else will do.

Glitter powder can be applied to fabrics where an outline of glue has been laid. Mark the design with glue and, before it dries, sprinkle silver or coloured glitter powder over the surface. Press gently with the fingers and leave to dry. Shake off loose powder onto a sheet of paper to use again. Glitter pens are available in which the glue and glitter powder are combined in a tube which acts like a pen. There are several different makes of these, eg Slickwriter or Gutermann Dekor.

Hard parts

Some of the dolls and puppets in this book have parts made not from cloth but from ceramic substitute Fimo (Polyform), which is really a kind of plastic material modelled whilst soft then hardened in an ordinary oven.

Both easy and clean to use, it is very popular though a little expensive. Instructions come with the packet but a few tips may be appreciated.

Though the material is sold in a variety of colours, including white and transparent, choose transparent over white as it is easier to handle. As white tends to go 'grey' during handling it has to be painted anyway so no time is gained. Fimo can be rolled out and cut into shapes with a craft knife, an apple corer or thimble. Flatten the Fimo out between two sheets of writing paper. Try to keep your fingernails as short as possible when working with Fimo as it marks very easily in its soft state. Details on small items can be sculpted with cocktail sticks and pencil ends.

There are other 'air-drying' clays on the market which may be useful but these tend to be rather heavy. One of the cheapest and most satisfying modelling materials can be made without leaving the kitchen. Flour, salt and water can be mixed to a dry rolling consistency and kneaded into shape just like clay. Use the following proportions: 450g (1lb) plain flour, 225g (½lb) salt and 300ml (½pt) cold water. This dough is really tough and hardwearing when dry and can be painted and varnished. The large amount of salt in the mixture stops it from going mouldy and, even though it tastes awful, a young child will not be harmed by licking it. Conventional clay can be used and fired in a kiln but the proportions of the cloth parts of the dolls will need to be changed as clay shrinks during firing. Another material that is worth trying is balsa wood. This can be bought in chunks meant for model airplane bodies but it can be carved and sanded into shape for puppet parts.

Painting and decorating

The best type of paint for Fimo and other plastics is the kind sold for painting model cars. It is a quick drying cellulose paint and comes in a variety of colours including some lovely metallic shades. Use a soft paintbrush to apply. Avoid using aerosols as these are dangerous and wasteful.

During painting it is easier to mount pieces on lumps of Plasticine (plastilene) to avoid leaving fingermarks. Supported firmly on Plasticine a piece can be dipped in paint for an ultra smooth covering, letting the paint run off onto newspaper. Make sure the piece is secure before dipping as there is nothing worse than watching a little component sinking into the paint. To dip parts with holes in them tie a length of cotton in a loop through the hole, suspend the part in the paint pot then hang it up to drip-dry over newspaper. A flat stick propped between two books provides a good hanger. For details use a fine marker pen in the appropriate colour or buy stickers – red dots for cheeks, black dots for eyes – and place them over the undercoat before varnishing.

When painting wood the best sort of paint is oil-based gloss over an undercoat. Make sure the wood is smooth. Sand off any sharp edges then paint all over with undercoat and leave to dry. Don't rush but leave plenty of time for each coat to dry thoroughly. Most paints now are non-toxic but check to make sure before using them on toys for children.

To paint wooden beads a good trick is to use a plastic golf tee to support the individual bead. Use the golf tee upside down with the wide end as a stand. Draw the features on the undercoated bead, first with pencil then with fine marker pen. If you make a mistake on one bead it can always be re-dipped in undercoat to start again.

When painted parts are completely dry they need to be varnished. A clear polyurethane varnish applied in two or three coats is very good but for small parts, eg beads etc, the most useful is a bottle of transparent nail lacquer. It is quick drying, non-toxic, thick covering and comes with its own little brush. Always let varnished parts dry in a dust-free room and don't disturb until the last coat is dry.

Patent nose (Fig 16)

This is a nose incorporated in the face to give shape to an otherwise flat plane. It is best used with a stretch material such as stockinette.

1 Cut the shape in double stockinette. Mark the circle of the nose in position on the RS of the top layer.
2 Stitch round on the outline using flesh-coloured embroidery thread in a small back stitch.
3 Make a tiny snip in the bottom layer at the centre of the circle and through this push a little pinch of toy filler or cotton wool (surgical cotton).
4 Stitch up the slit and back the middle of the face with interfacing ready for embroidery.

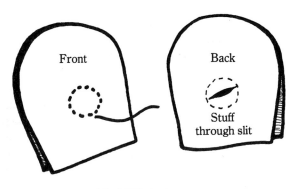

Fig 16 Patent nose

To make eyes (Fig 17)

The 'pie-slice eye' is an effective eye for a cloth doll.

1 Cut circles of felt the required diameter, 2 in black and 2 in white. The easiest way is to put dot stickers of the right size onto the felt and cut round them. Discard the stickers.
2 Cut a pie-slice out of the black felts and place each one over a white circle.
3 Place them on the face and either glue them or stitch them down with the white slices at the same angle on each eye. If crosses are desired over the eyes make 4 big stitches into the middle of each eye extending about 1cm (½in) beyond the rim.

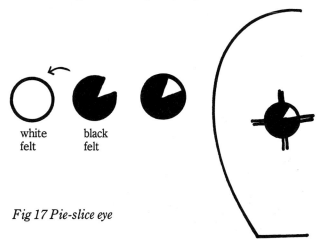

white felt
black felt

Fig 17 Pie-slice eye

Very small felt eyes can be punched out of felt with an ordinary office punch (hole punch). These eyes should be glued to the faces of small toys. Some of the dolls' faces can be given more contours by 'sinking' the eyes when the head is made up and stuffed (see Fig 18). To do this pass a long needle threaded with black thread, from the back of the doll's head to one eye, down to the corner of the mouth below it, then back again to the

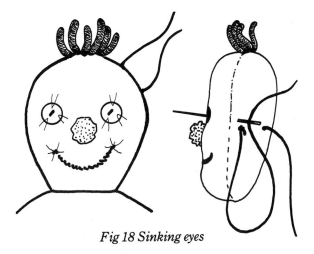

Fig 18 Sinking eyes

back of the head. Leave the remaining thread trailing. Do the same for the other side. Pull up the trailing threads so the face puckers, then tie the threads together tightly. The knot will be hidden under the doll's hair or hat. Where this method is not practical work entirely on the face. Anchor the thread with small stitches at one corner of the mouth, pass the needle up to the eye above, then across to the other eye and down to the matching corner of the mouth. Pull the thread tightly and anchor it here with small stitches. Squeeze the head into shape.

To make hair (Fig 19)

Different thicknesses of yarn are used for different dolls but all are attached in the same way. For the bald wig (see page 118) a thick rug wool, chunky or double knitting wool for the middle sized dolls and stranded embroidery thread for the tiny ones. In most cases the strands of yarn are set into a seam for strength.

1 Wind the yarn round a book or strong card which is half the measured strand. Cut the yarn along one side.
2 Place the lengths over the seam line where they will lie, with the seam line halfway down the strands.
3 Sew along on the seam line over the strands.

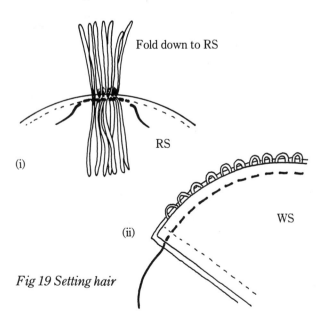

Fig 19 Setting hair

4 Fold the strands back onto the fabric, exposing the SA. Hold them out of the way with Sellotape.
5 Place the part to be joined over the hair seam, RS tog, and sew along the seam including the folded edges of the yarn in the stitching.
6 Trim the hair to a uniform length before finishing the doll.

Tassels (Fig 20)

1 Wind the yarn round a book or stiff card about the width of finished tassels' length.
2 Pass a thread under the loops and tie it tightly.
3 Cut the opposite side of the loops to release.
4 Wind a piece of the yarn round the strands about 25mm (1in) from the top. Tie the ends and, with a bodkin, pass them through the body of the tassel.
5 Trim the ends level.

Fig 20 Making tassels

Pompons (Fig 21)

Bought pompons are safer than home-made ones as their threads are less likely to come out. Pompons are an indispensible item when making any sort of clown so it is as well to give them some attention. Always buy the right size for the doll and try to get a good colour match with other materials. If pompons are impossible to find you will have to make your own. The following method is almost fool-proof: To make a pompon of about 5cm (2in) diam.

1 Cut two circles of stiff card with holes in the middle. To do this use a set of compasses. First draw a circle with 1cm (³⁄₈in) radius, then draw a wider circle, from the same point, with 25mm (1in) radius. Cut out the cards and remove the inner circles.
2 Cut long lengths of the chosen yarn and wind them round both circles put together, passing the yarn through the centre space each time (see Fig 21).

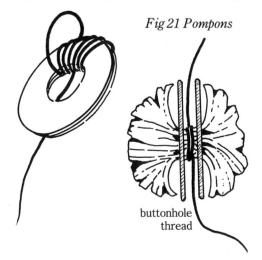

Fig 21 Pompons

buttonhole thread

3 Wind the yarn as thickly as space allows so the pompon will not be straggly.

4 When the card is as full as can be, cut the outer edge with scissors going down into the cleft between the cards.

5 Pull the cards slightly apart and pass a length of buttonhole thread (buttonhole twist) round the middle of the pompon. Tie 3 knots tightly in the thread.

6 Tear away the cards and fluff up the pompon so the thread is hidden. Trim the pompon evenly all over, cutting down to size if necessary.

Most pompons fail because the centre tie is made with the same yarn as the pompon and it usually stretches. Buttonhole thread, well-knotted, holds the strands better.

Frills

Double-folded frill (Fig 22)

This can be made out of contrasting fabric or self fabric. It doesn't have an outer hem but is rather bulky at the gathering edge making it unsuitable for use with thick fabrics.

1 Cut the length and width of fabric required. Fold the piece in half, RS tog, and sew the side seam.

2 Fold the fabric WS tog along the whole of its length and press the edge.

3 Gather on the seam line and pull the gathers up to form the frill.

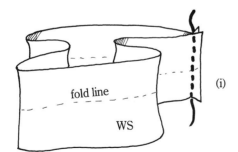

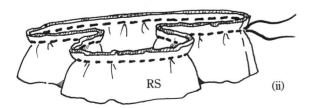

Fig 22 Double-folded frill

Ribbon frills

1 Cut length of ribbon required and form a circle with ends overlapping about 1cm (½in).

2 Glue the overlap and leave to dry.

3 Run a gathering thread along one edge, very close to the edge.

4 Place the frill where it belongs on the doll and pull up the gathers to fit tightly. (NB For wide ribbon join the neck frill with a French seam rather than glue (see page 16).)

Puff frill (Fig 23)

This is a very useful frill to know as it can be made in sizes from very tiny to extremely large. The best fabrics to use are non-fraying types, eg dress net and nylon, but as the frill is cut in a circle fraying is minimal anyway.

1 Cut out the circle in the required size. Note that the frill is cut twice as large in diameter as the finished frill will be.

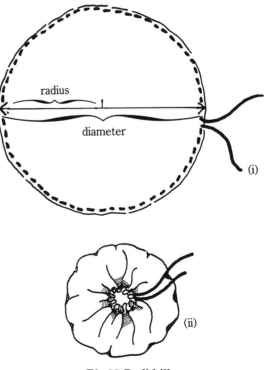

Fig 23 Puff frill

2 Run a gathering thread all the way round the edge of the circle.

3 Pull the gathers tight into the middle.

4 Anchor the gathering thread. Finish off and press the frill lightly by hand.

5 If necessary cut a slit in the lower layer of the frill opposite the centre point.

Three-piece boot (Fig 24)

This is a smart little boot for a doll.

1 Cut the pieces carefully, two sides and one oval sole.
2 With RS tog, join the curved upper seam. Clip the SA.
3 Mark the points CF and CB on the sole and pin the sole to the uppers matching CF, RS tog. Sew round each side as far as CB.
4 Fold boot, RS tog, and sew back seam.

When stuffing boots put equal amounts of toy filler in each one. Fill the boots alternately, a pinch at a time, rather than fill one boot completely followed by the other.

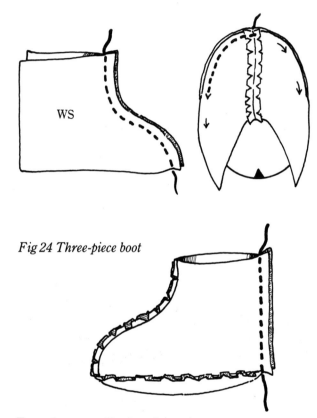

Fig 24 Three-piece boot

French seam (Enclosed seam)

This is a good seam to use when joining friable fabrics. Place the parts to be joined WS tog and sew on a line half way within the SA. Trim the SA down close to the stitching and open out the fabric. Fold the fabric RS tog and make another line of stitching on the seam line.

Stuffing

Soft toys need to be stuffed carefully to give the fabrics a good feel and shape. Almost every fibre, seed or feather has been used as a stuffing in the past from duck-down to sawdust. Nowadays there are lots of good, clean materials to choose from and each is as good as another when used appropriately. Kapok, a vegetable fibre, is lovely and soft inside a cushion. Little dolls can be filled with potpourri, dried rose petals or lavender seeds when they are for decoration only, and small areas can be stuffed successfully with cotton wool. Synthetic sponge chip is an inexpensive filling for large objects but do check for fire safety first. Dolls which are to be given to children should be filled with flame retardant polyester filler carrying the British Standard Mark or equivalent. This is especially important if the toys are made for re-sale.

FINISHING TOUCHES

To ensure a pleasing result, press your work, at stages throughout, with a warm or hot iron and give a final press when it is finished. Starch and iron any limp fabrics or ribbons before using them. Trim pompons and hair carefully and pick up stray bits of thread and fluff with a piece of Sellotape (Scotchtape) wound round the hand, sticky side out. Tie bows crisply and cut off the ends at an angle to stop the ribbon fraying.

SAFETY

When making toys and playthings for young children always be alert to the possibilities of harmful components (the same applies when *buying* toys). Leave off hard attachments, such as bells, on any toys for the use of children under three years old. Bought pompons are safer than home-made ones as they do not shred as easily, but make sure that both kinds are fastened on securely. Give each one a good tug as a test.

When making dolls, use best-quality sewing thread and make strong seams with back stitch if sewing by hand. Use a safe, hygienic filling (see above), in anything destined for a child. If your particular child is allergic to wool you should use knitting cotton (candlewick) for the hair and wigs and choose designs that will machine wash, or wash easily.

HAND OR MACHINE

BEAN BAG

This tough action clown is suitable for children of three years and upwards. He will fly through the air and, still smiling, land on the floor with a satisfying thud. Make him in strong, bright cotton or, for an older child, from suede leather off-cuts, in which case omit the SA on the pattern pieces except at the neck edge of the head and the top edge of the feet and hands. Sew suede as you would felt, with WS tog and stitching close to the edge. Use thin strips of leather instead of wool for the hair and paint or stick features onto the face instead of embroidering them.

MATERIALS

10cm (4in) square of flesh-coloured felt
Enough bright red felt to make a
    small triangle for a nose
25cm (10in) square of bright
patterned red and white cotton
25×35cm (10×14in) piece of plain cotton in a
    contrasting colour (eg blue)
30cm (12in) square of plain cotton in a third
    colour (eg yellow)
Approx 6m (5½yd) bright red rug wool
A large handful of toy stuffing
Approx 500g (1lb) lentils
80cm (32in) of red satin ribbon 4cm (1½in)
    wide
50cm (20in) of blue satin ribbon 4cm
    (1½in) wide
Embroidery thread in red, black, white
    and blue
Sewing thread to match fabrics

METHOD

1 Make the pattern
    (see page 18). The SA
    on the pattern pieces
    varies: 1cm (½in) allowed
    on A and B all round and on
    wrist and ankle edges of C and D. The curved
    edges of C and D have ½cm (¼in).

2 Cut out piece A once in flesh felt and once in blue cotton.
3 Cut out piece B once in red fabric and once in blue.
4 Cut out piece C 4 times (2 pairs) in yellow.
5 Cut out piece D 4 times (2 pairs) in yellow.
6 Cut a small triangle of red felt for the nose.
7 Cut the wool for the hair into 25 strands each 20cm (8in) long.
8 Transfer pattern markings to fabrics.

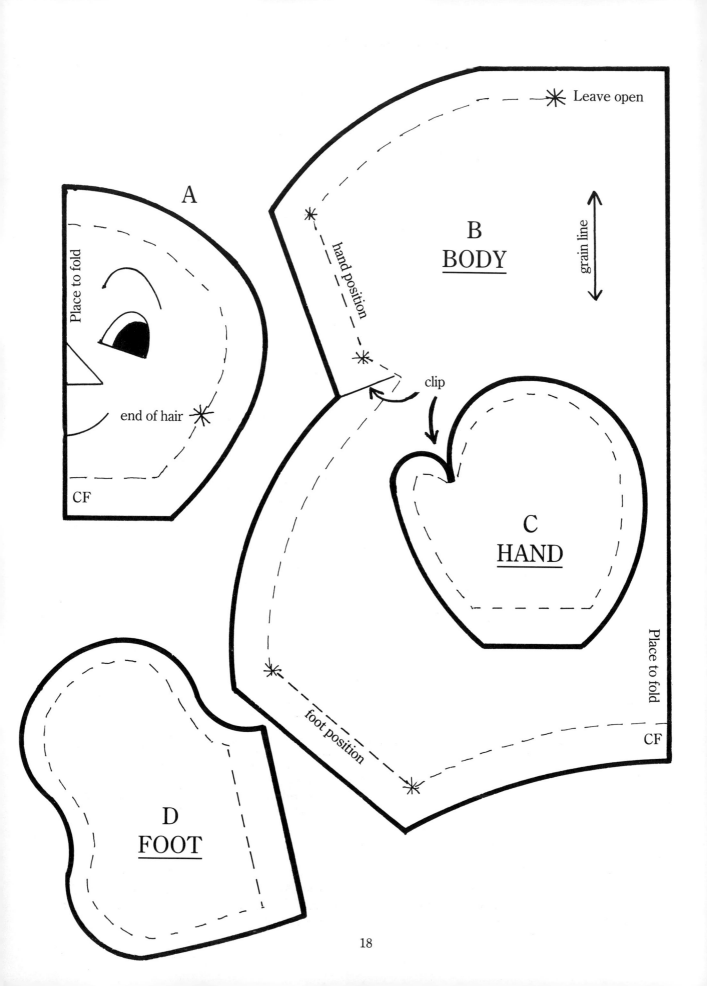

A

Place to fold

end of hair

CF

B
BODY

Leave open

grain line

hand position

clip

C
HAND

Place to fold

CF

foot position

D
FOOT

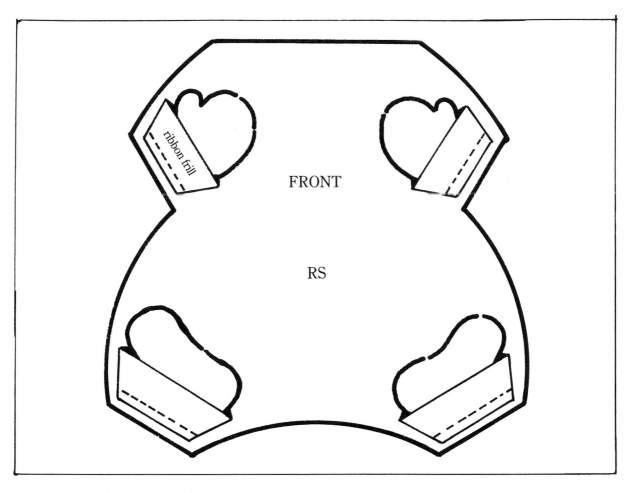

FRONT

RS

ribbon frill

Fig 1 Position of hands and feet on front of suit

Head

1 Sew nose in place on face.
2 Using satin stitch, embroider eyes in black and white.
3 Using stem stitch, embroider mouth line in black.
4 Apply wool to hair line (see page 14).
5 Place back of head and face RS tog and sew round enclosing hair and leaving neck edge open.
6 Turn out and stuff the head lightly. Close off the neck opening on the seam line.

Hands and feet

1 Place hands and feet in pairs RS tog.
2 Sew round leaving openings at wrist and ankle edges.
3 Turn out. Stuff. Close up openings on seam line.
4 Cut the red ribbon into 4 lengths of 20cm (8in). Make 4 ribbon frills (see page 15).
5 Place the frills over the hands and feet so the join in the ribbon will be at the back and not at the edge. Sew across on the seam line through all layers. (NB Put a small rubber band round each frill to help keep it out of the way during sewing.)

Body

1 Sew hands and feet in position on front of suit (see Fig 1).
2 Place body sections RS tog and sew all round except for neck opening. Take care where seams thicken over hands and feet.
3 Clip SA at place marked.
4 Turn out. Check that frills have not got caught up in the seams and that the seam is intact. If in doubt sew round again (remember it has to hold lentils).
5 Press the SA to the inside at the opening.
6 Fill the body bag with the lentils.
7 Push the head into the neck opening and top-stitch across. The head is meant to be floppy and the body baggy.

To finish

1 Trim the hair evenly to 6cm (2½in).
2 Make a bow out of the blue ribbon and place at CF neck. Sew by hand at each side of the knot through to the back of the neck.

GYMNAST

This amusing toy is common to most cultures. Known as the Acrobat or Gymnast, its movement depends on tension strings relaxing and tightening to send the small figure tumbling head over heels.

The wood for the frame must be flexible but not so thin as to break under hand pressure – beading is ideal. The centre joint of the frame is a piece of garden cane which is the cheapest, most easily found, hollow tube of wood. Thin pieces of wood have a tendency to split when pierced so making the doll's arms from modelling material overcomes this problem.

As an alternative to painting the frame yellow leave the wood plain and just use varnish. For a continental look decorate the struts with simple motifs such as hearts or flowers by painting or using transfers before applying the varnish. For painting wood and beads, see page 13.

MATERIALS

For the frame:
2 pieces of half-round beading 25mm (1in) wide×30cm (12in) long
A piece of garden cane 6cm (2½in) long, about 1cm (½in) diam
2 round-headed brass screws 2cm (¾in) with rawlplugs
Glasspaper in medium and fine grains
White undercoat
Bright yellow gloss
Clear varnish

For the doll:
1 wooden bead 25mm (1in) diam, painted white (for head)
1 bead 1cm (½in) diam (for head stop)
2 beads 2cm (¾in) diam, painted black (for feet)
2 beads 1cm (½in) diam, painted black (for foot stops)
White paint, black paint, clear varnish
Fine marker pens in red, black and white
2 round red stickers 5mm (¼in) diam

1 wine cork 25mm (1in) diam×4cm (1½in) long
A finger cut from an old red knitted glove
¼ block of red Fimo modelling material
Copydex adhesive
30cm (12in) bright tartan ribbon 25mm (1in) wide
8cm (3in) square of yellow felt
25cm (10in) bright green satin ribbon 8cm (3in) wide
Embroidery threads in green and yellow
Approx 1m (1yd) red knitting cotton or thin string

Use of:
1cm (½in) wide paintbrush
Turpentine for brush cleaning
Plasticine modelling clay and plastic golf tees for supports during painting
Various small tools; screwdriver, bradawl, craft saw, craft knife, hammer and pliers.

METHOD

Making the arms
1 Make a template of paper by tracing off Fig 1.
2 Cut Fimo into two halves.
3 Flatten each half into a sausage shape 5mm (¼in) thick, cut round using template and mark holes with a pin.
4 Enlarge the holes to take the string easily. Mark the hand line with the back of a knife.
5 Place both arms on a baking tray and bake as directed.
6 When cool run a loop of thread through the top hole and dip in white paint as far as the hand line. Suspend freely to dry.
7 When completely dry dip the whole arm in varnish and hang up again to dry. Make sure the holes are not blocked with varnish.

hand end

Fig 1 Arm template (actual size)

Making the doll

1 Paint and varnish the beads using Fig 2 for the features.

Fig 2 Enlarged view of face

2 Cut the cork in half across. Use one half only.

3 Push the cork into the glove finger and gather up the raw end tightly.

4 Join head to body as in Fig 3 by weaving the thread in and out of the knitted glove finger. There is no need to pass through the cork itself. Use a fairly large needle and a piece of the red cotton but see that the needle will go through the holes in the beads. Start at the base leaving about 5cm (2in) of cotton trailing. Go up CF. Pass through the head bead then through the stop bead. Go back through the head bead then down CB. Tie the two ends together in a firm knot. Dab the knot with glue.

5 To assemble the arms, use the same method but go round the body (see Fig 4). Pass the cotton through the shoulder hole in one arm leaving about 5cm (2in) trailing. Go horizontally through front of body and

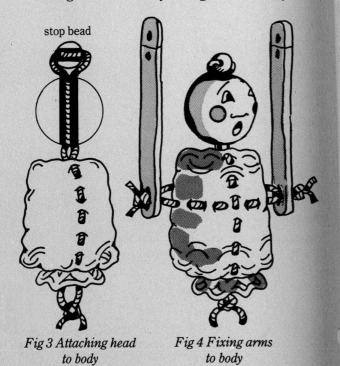

Fig 3 Attaching head   Fig 4 Fixing arms
    to body   to body

into shoulder hole of second arm leaving trailing same amount of cotton. Repeat this operation at the back of the body. Tie the cotton ends together at each side and dab the knots with glue.

6 Make neck frill of tartan ribbon and pull up round doll's neck (see page 15).

7 Cut hat shape from yellow felt using template made from Fig 5. Sew up CB close to edge. Turn up the brim a little all round. Spread a thin film of glue just inside the hat and stick it to the doll's head.

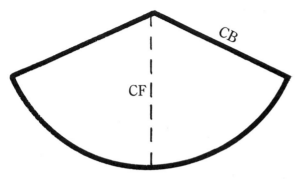

Fig 5 Hat template (actual size)

8 To make trousers, cut the green ribbon into two equal pieces one for each leg. Fold each piece across RS tog. Stitch up to the halfway point close to the edge. Join the two legs together. Turn out and run a gathering thread round the waist. Pull onto the doll's body and tighten the gathers. Attach the trousers to the body at waistline CB, CF and both sides.

9 Gather each ankle 1cm (½in) from the bottom edge and sew the bead feet in place. To do this first anchor a thread inside the frill, pass it through the bigger bead, through the stop bead, back through the bigger bead and anchor again inside the frill.

Making the frame

1 Using a bradawl, make holes in the pieces of beading as in Fig 6. Between top and point (a) there is a space of 25mm (1in). Between (a) and (b) there is a space of 1cm (½in). Between base and point (c) there is a space of 8cm (3in). Clean up the wood with glasspaper.

2 Cut a section of garden cane 6cm (2½in) long from a part of the cane where the diameter will be about 1cm (½in). Clean up with glasspaper.

3 Hammer rawlplugs into the ends of cane section.

4 Protecting the passive hand with a strong gardening glove, screw the cane cross-bar into position at (c) (holding the cane with pliers helps to steady it).

5 Clean up the screw heads with glasspaper.

6 Paint the frame or decorate as desired. During the painting make sure the holes stay free.

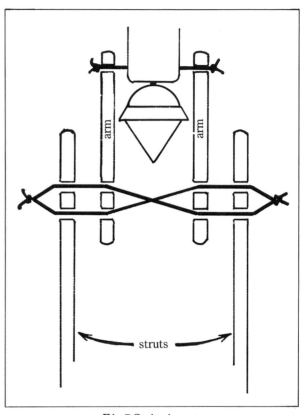

Fig 7 Stringing up

Stringing up (Fig 7)

The best method is to lay the doll between the struts of the frame with its head pointing towards the base. Line up the holes in his arms with the holes in the struts. Cut two pieces of red cotton or string 20cm (8in) long and lace them through the holes crossing over in the middle between the doll's hands. Tie the free ends together. Be prepared to adjust the knots until the correct amount of tension is achieved. Put the little fellow through his paces by gently squeezing the frame at its base. When satisfied with the action, tie the knots securely and dab with glue.

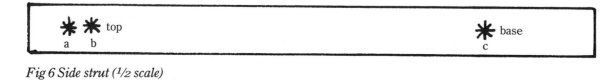

Fig 6 Side strut (½ scale)

PRAM RATTLE

This colourful rattle would be suitable for a baby of about six months. Hang it across the hood of the pram within reach of the child. Plastic kitten balls containing a bell can be bought cheaply from a pet shop but sometimes the plastic is rough in places. Before starting, clean up the balls with a sharp knife and hold any surface flaws against a warm iron to smooth them out. Young children put everything in their mouths so take care when purchasing fabrics and components for their toys.

MATERIALS

70cm (28in) thick cord elastic
6 white plastic beads or anorak cord ends
4 plastic kitten balls containing bells
13cm (5in) square of flesh felt
25cm (10in) square of red felt
A piece of green and white striped cotton fabric 60cm (24in) wide×40cm (16in) long
Embroidery threads in red, black, flesh, white and orange
White sewing thread
60cm (24in) red and white dotted ribbon 25mm (1in) wide (20cm (8in) for each clown)
90cm (36in) double-sided red satin ribbon 1cm (½in) wide (30cm (12in) for each clown)
2 handfuls of toy filling
Copydex adhesive
Use of a crochet hook for threading up

METHOD

1 Make pattern for the clown dolls (see page 24). (There is a SA of ½cm (¼in) all round pants piece B and at neck and ankle edge of E and D.)
2 Place top edge of piece A to a fold.
3 Cut out A 3 times in red felt.
4 Cut out C 3 times in red felt.
5 Cut out D 12 times in red felt.
6 Cut out E 6 times in flesh felt.

7 Cut out B 12 times (6 pairs) in green stripe.
8 Transfer features and pattern markings to fabrics.
9 Cut slit at neck on A as marked.
10 Embroider features on 3 faces.

To make 1 clown

1 Place face and back of head WS tog.
2 Sew round close to the edge leaving open at base.
3 Stuff head and sew across neck on seam line.
4 Fold hat cone and sew up the back close to the edge.
5 Turn up the brim and sew hat to doll's head with small unobtrusive stitches.
6 Using orange embroidery thread make hair loops at sides of head, 3 loops each side.
7 Using white embroidery thread make tassel at hat point. (Make a small, tight stitch between each looped stitch to prevent the thread pulling out.)
8 Push the made-up head into the neck opening of the suit and sew across on the seam line through all layers (Fig 1).

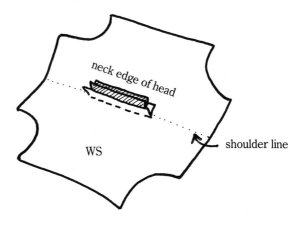

Fig 1 Joining head to suit

9 Fold back the suit and sew underarm seams close to edge.
10 Sew boot sections together in pairs stitching close to the edge.
11 Place 4 pants sections, RS tog in pairs. Sew inside leg seams and side seams. Turn out 1 leg.
12 Slip 1 leg inside the other RS tog, and sew round crotch seam. Turn out to WS.

13 Gather leg openings to fit tops of boots.

14 Push boots into leg openings from inside, toes towards side seams, and sew across openings through all layers.

15 Turn out and stuff the legs lightly.

16 Gather pants waist to fit suit waist.

17 Push pants into suit and top-stitch across waistline.

18 Make neck frill from spotted ribbon and fasten tightly round doll's neck (see page 15).

19 Cut waist ribbon and fasten at CB waistline with small stitches. Tie in a bow at CF. Trim ends of ribbon to points.

Assembly

1 Thread the beads, balls and clowns onto the elastic in the following order: first ball, white bead, clown, white bead, ball, white bead, clown, white bead, ball, white bead, clown, white bead, ball (see illustration on page 7).

2 Using a weaver's knot, make loops at each end of the elastic. Adjust the length to fit the pram width. (NB A little dab of glue on the white beads will hold them into the sleeve ends.)

3 Make sure the rattle will not come unthreaded when pulled.

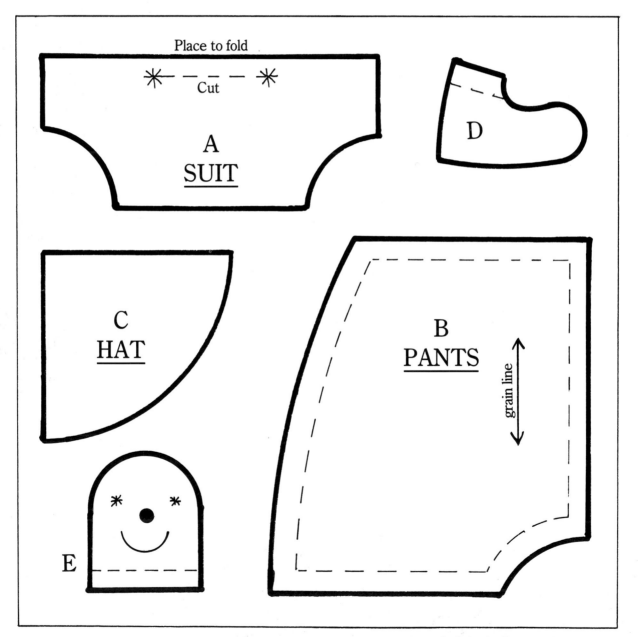

Jack-in-the-Box and Pram Rattle

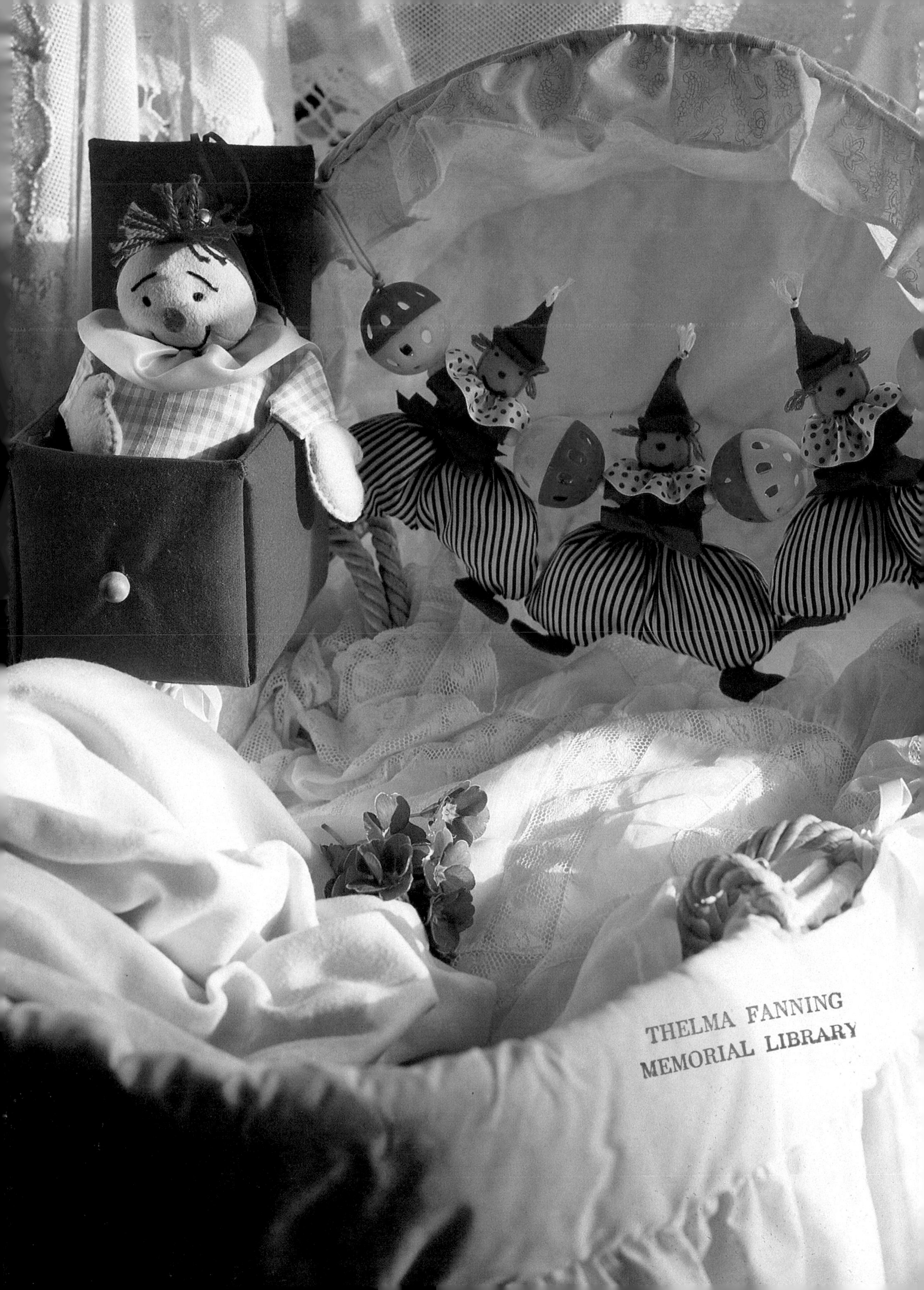

JACK-IN-THE-BOX

This cute clown is based on the traditional boxed toy using the element of surprise. This soft version has no harmful metal spring inside but gets its jump from compressed sponges and recoiling elastic. The box is soft and requires no woodworking ability – squares of hardboard can be cut to order from most wood suppliers or DIY shops. Cheap, synthetic bath sponges are ideal for the body filling. Cut them roughly with sharp scissors.

MATERIALS

For the box

6 pieces of hardboard 10cm (4in) square, 5mm (¼in) thick
46cm (18in) polyester wadding 92cm (36in) wide
30cm (12in) bright pink strong cotton fabric 92cm (36in) wide
40cm (16in) bright pink satin ribbon 2.5mm (⅛in) wide
1 'bobble' button
Bright pink buttonhole thread

For the doll:

23cm (9in) square of flesh felt
A small circle of bright pink felt 1cm (½in) diam
28cm (11in) royal blue satin ribbon 8cm (3in) wide
A piece of yellow and white small check gingham 25×46cm (10×18in)
A flat button 25mm (1in) diam
40cm (16in) white satin ribbon 5cm (2in) wide
Embroidery thread in flesh, blue, black and white
Sewing thread to match suit
Bright pink knitting cotton – 10 strands, each 10cm (4in) long
A tiny gold bell about 1cm (½in) diam
Copydex adhesive
Sellotape
12cm (4½in) elastic 1cm (½in) wide
4 sponge discs 5cm (2in) thick, 6cm (2½in) diam
1 handful of toy filling

TO MAKE THE BOX

Construction

Cut the wadding into 6 squares, 22cm (8½in) sq.

Cut pink fabric into 12 squares, 14cm (4½in) sq.

Spread Copydex on smooth sides of hardboards and pad each one with wadding.

1 Place hardboard glue side down in centre of wadding (see Fig 1).
2 Fold corners of wadding to centre of board (trim if necessary).
3 Fold opposite corners of wadding into centre and secure with stitches along the diagonals (Fig 1).
4 Place pink fabric squares in pairs RS tog.

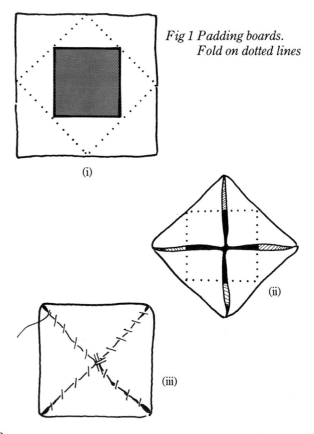

Fig 1 Padding boards. Fold on dotted lines

(i)

(ii)

(iii)

For 4 sides

1 Take 4 pairs of squares and sew round 3 sides of each with 1cm (½in) SA.
2 Clip the corners, turn out and press.
3 Insert the padded boards into each 'pocket' and sew across open end on the seam line (see Fig 2).

For base

1 Sandwich 1 padded board between 2 pink squares and tack round on the seam line all round. (NB The thicker side of the padded board is the outer side of the box except on the base.)
2 Join the sides to the base. Place raw edges of base and 4 sides together with sides hanging free. Sew across each one on the seam line (see Fig 2).

For the lid

1 Make a loop of the narrow pink ribbon and sew it into the centre of the top edge seam when joining the last pair of pink squares. Position the loop so that it hangs outwards when the pocket is turned and includes a good 5cm (2in) inside. Sew round the 3 sides as before going over the enclosed ribbon a couple of times to secure.
2 Clip the corners, turn out and press.
3 Insert the last padded board and tuck in the SA at the open edge.
4 Oversew the opening.
5 Oversew the lid to the back edge of the box (see Fig 3). (Don't sew up the sides yet as the next step is to make the doll.)

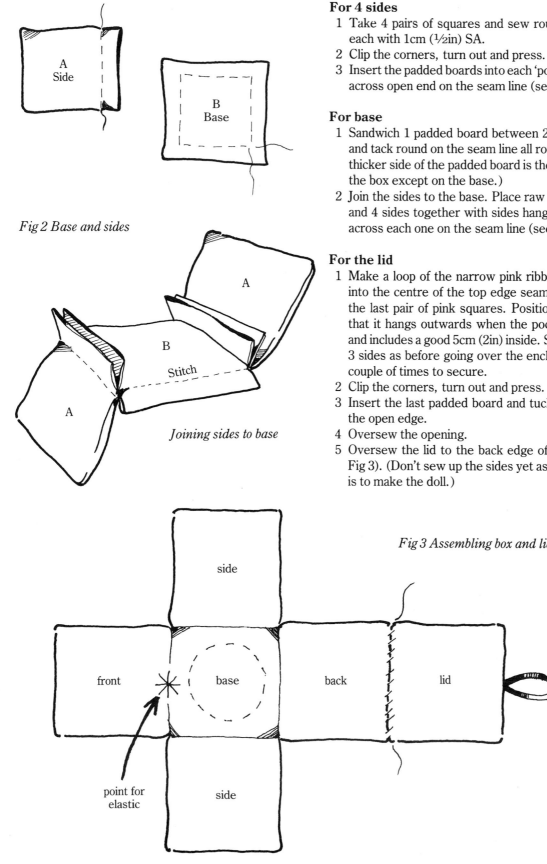

Fig 2 Base and sides

Joining sides to base

Fig 3 Assembling box and lid

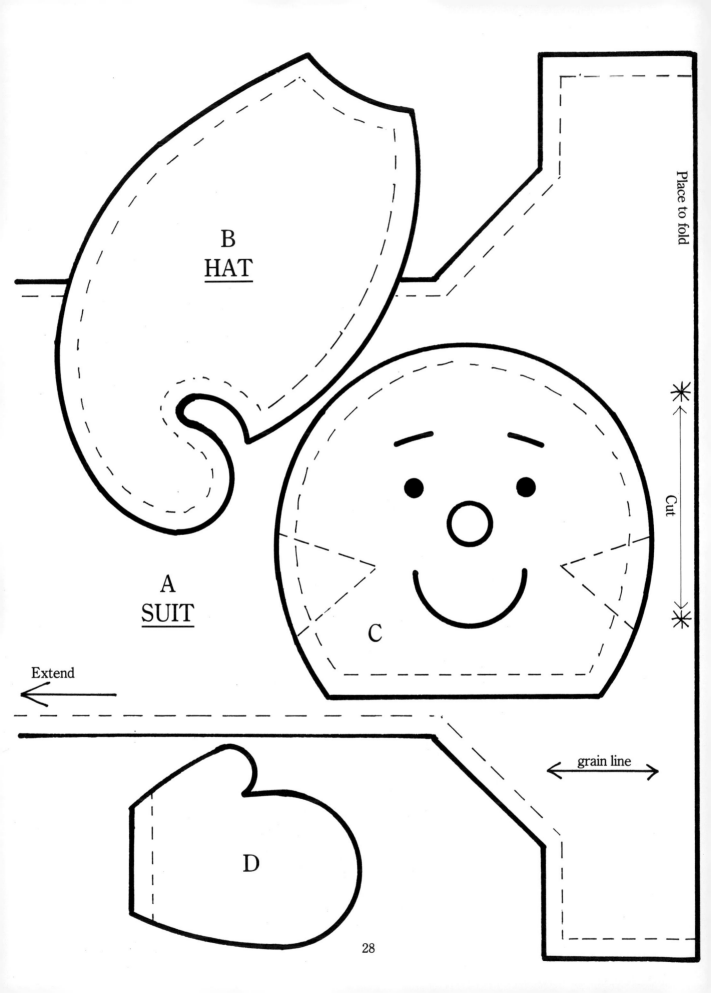

B
HAT

A
SUIT

C

D

Place to fold

Cut

Extend

grain line

28

To make the doll

1 Make the pattern (opposite). (NB The bottom edge of the suit needs to be extended for 4cm (1½in). There is a SA of ½cm (¼in) everywhere except on the curve of the hand. The pattern piece for the hat must be reversed on the blue satin ribbon to make a pair. Lay out the suit pattern with the top edge on the fold of material.)
2 Cut out A once in yellow check folded in half.
3 Cut out B twice from blue satin ribbon.
4 Cut out C once from flesh felt.
5 Cut out D 4 times from flesh felt.
6 Transfer features and pattern markings to fabrics.

Face

1 Stick nose in place.
2 Using stem stitch and French knots, embroider the eyes, mouth and eyebrows with black embroidery thread.
3 Make darts in cheeks.
4 Make hair with knitting cotton and stitch to face at CF.

Hat

1 Place hat pieces RS tog.
2 Sew round back seam.
3 Clip SA. Turn out. Poke out the point carefully.

To join hat to face

1 Place hat and face RS tog.
2 Sew round face seam including hair in seam.
3 Turn out and stuff fairly tightly.
4 Close up the opening at the neck by running a gathering thread round the edge and pulling up tight.
5 Sink the eyes (see pages 13-14).
6 Sew bell to point of hat and trim fringe to eye level.

To make neck stop

1 Cut 2 felt circles slightly larger than the button.
2 Sandwich the button between them and stab-stitch all round.
3 Sew the doll's head to the neck stop (see Fig 4 overleaf).

Suit

1 Cut neck opening.
2 Fold suit over, RS tog, and sew round leaving open at base, neck and sleeve ends.
3 Turn out. Press SA to inside at base, neck and sleeves.

Hands

1 Place hands in pairs and sew round close to edge leaving wrists open.
2 Stuff hands and sew across wrist at seam line.
3 Push hands into ends of sleeves (thumbs up) and top-stitch across.

To join head to body

1 Run a gathering thread round the neck edge of the suit starting at CB.
2 Insert the doll's head and pull the gathers up tightly enclosing the button stop.
3 Make neck frill from the white satin ribbon (see page 15).

To assemble the toy

Before completing the box the doll must be spring loaded without actually using a spring (see Fig 5).

1 Leave the sleeves of the suit unstuffed but fill the body with the sponge discs stacked up inside. Run a gathering thread round the base of the suit and pull up tightly to enclose the sponges.

2 Sew one end of the elastic to the base of the box at CF inside.
3 Lay the elastic flat across the base of the box and position the doll on top of the elastic.
4 Sew the suit to the base of the box at each side of the elastic.
5 Pass the elastic up the back of the doll, stretching it so it reaches the doll's shoulders and pressing the doll down at the same time (another pair of hands may be needed for this operation).
6 Keeping the elastic in place, fasten it firmly to the suit. When the doll is bent forcibly forwards then released the elastic should pull him up sharply. To enhance this effect the inside surfaces of the box can be covered with Sellotape to make them shiny. This is especially useful if the fabric of the box creates a lot of drag on the doll.

To finish the box

1 Fold up the sides of the box round the doll.
2 Sew the top corners together securely and the box will keep upright; there is no need to sew down each side to the base.
3 Squash the doll down inside the box and close the lid.
4 Mark where the button needs to be on the front and sew it in place.
5 Make a loop in the ribbon so it fastens easily over the button.

Fig 4 Joining doll's head and neck stop

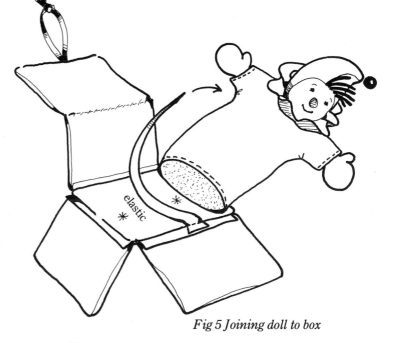

Fig 5 Joining doll to box

PUNCH AND JUDY

These two hand puppets are based on the traditional knockabout characters seen at seaside resorts. The short morality play they act out has different popular versions but all end with the main character, the bullying and egotistical Mr Punch, getting his come-uppance.

The dolls are simple and attractive in their own right but can be made more elaborate if desired. If you are lucky enough to find a large cardboard box of the type that fridges and washing machines are delivered in, you can make a booth for staging a show. Cut away part of the front at the top and either cover the card with red and white striped cloth or paint stripes with a wide brush. A makeshift stage can be made by draping a cloth over a line stretched across a doorway.

The hand puppets are best worked by putting the forefinger into the head with the thumb up one sleeve and the second finger up the other.

MATERIALS

For Punch
A piece of flesh felt 18cm×25cm (7×10in)
2 circles of pink felt 2cm (³⁄₄in) diam
Green felt 33×12cm (13×5in)
White felt 30×15cm (12×6in)
Red velvet 40cm (16in) wide×50cm (20in) long
6m (6yd) white rug wool cut into 12 pieces, each 50cm (20in) long
6 round gold-coloured bells 1cm (¹⁄₂in) diam
50cm (20in) black satin ribbon 1cm (¹⁄₂in) wide

For Judy
A piece of double flesh stockinette 10cm (4in) square
Blue and white check cotton fabric 25×50cm (10×20in)
Bright yellow cotton fabric 35×40cm (14×16in)
2 circles of black felt 5mm (¹⁄₄in) diam
150cm (2yd) brown rug wool cut into 6 pieces, each 25cm (10in) long
50cm (20in) blue satin ribbon 1cm (¹⁄₂in) wide

Iron-on interfacing 25×18cm (10×7in)
2 decorative buttons

For baby
Some paper lace or a cake doily
A wooden lolly stick
White thin ribbon or finger bandage
Approx 30cm (12in) white, pink or blue satin ribbon 1cm (¹⁄₂in) wide

For all
Stiff card, chocolate-box weight (see Fig 1 for cutting)
35cm (14in) white broderie anglaise (eyelet) edging 25mm (1in) wide
Sellotape
Copydex adhesive
2 handfuls of toy filler
A fine-line black marker
Embroidery threads in black, white, pink, flesh-pink red and green
Sewing threads in red, yellow and blue

METHOD

1 Make patterns for both puppets (see pages 34-5). (NB There is a SA of ¹⁄₂cm (¹⁄₄in) on all pieces except on the curve of the hand. When cutting out the felt frills extend the ends ¹⁄₂cm (¹⁄₄in) into an overlap. Extend base of suit pattern 6cm (2¹⁄₂in).
2 Cut out A from folded fabric once in blue check and once in red velvet.
3 Cut B once in yellow fabric.
4 Cut D once in yellow fabric.
5 Cut C twice in yellow fabric and once in interfacing.
6 Cut E 4 times in white felt.
7 Cut H twice in red velvet.
8 Cut K once on double stockinette.
9 Cut I twice (one pair) in flesh felt.
10 Cut J twice (one pair) in flesh felt.
11 To make the cape frill, fold pattern paper 5 times. Draw F once on top layer and cut through with side of section against folded edge. Cut F once in green felt.

12 To make the hat frill, do the same as for the cape frill but only on 4 folds of paper. Cut G once in green felt. The raw fabric edges inside the bodies will need finishing off with oversewing or pinking shears. This can be done first.

13 Transfer pattern markings to fabrics.

To assemble bodies

1 Make hands in pairs sewing round close to edge and leaving wrist edge open.
2 Cut neck openings in bodies.
3 Turn up a narrow hem at the wrists of the suits.
4 Add broderie anglaise trim to Judy's suit at sleeve ends.
5 Fold suits RS tog and sew underarm seams.
6 Turn out the suits and make a narrow hem at the base of each.
7 Make card inserts to fit inside the hands and hold with a dab of glue (Fig 1).
8 Push hands into sleeve ends up to the felt edge. Sew round by hand (thumbs point upwards).

Fig 1 Making hands

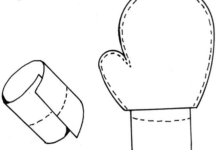

Judy's head

1 Make patent nose on the face (see page 13).
2 Treat double stockinette as one piece and embroider the mouth in pink thread. Stick the black felt eyes in place and make 3 stitches in black thread at the top of each one.
3 Stay-stitch round perimeter of face on seam line.

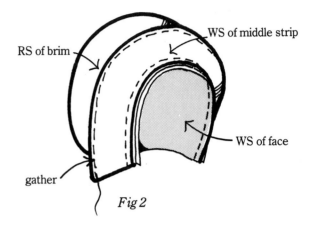

WS of middle strip

RS of brim

WS of face

gather

Fig 2

Judy's bonnet

1 Iron interfacing to back of one brim piece.
2 Place brims RS tog. Sew round outer curve.
3 Turn out and press firmly.
4 Sew brim to middle section RS tog. Then sew both to the edge of the face (see Fig 2).
5 Gather other edge of middle section to fit bonnet back.
6 Place RS tog and sew round.
7 Turn out and stuff lightly.

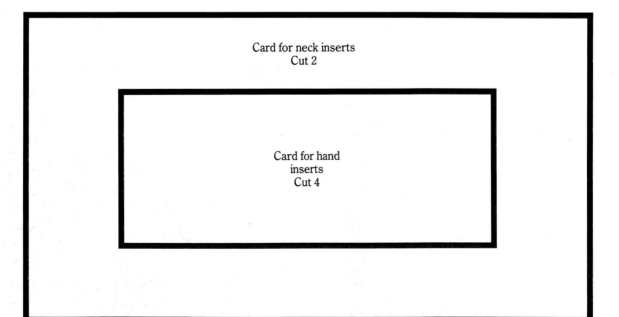

Card for neck inserts
Cut 2

Card for hand
inserts
Cut 4

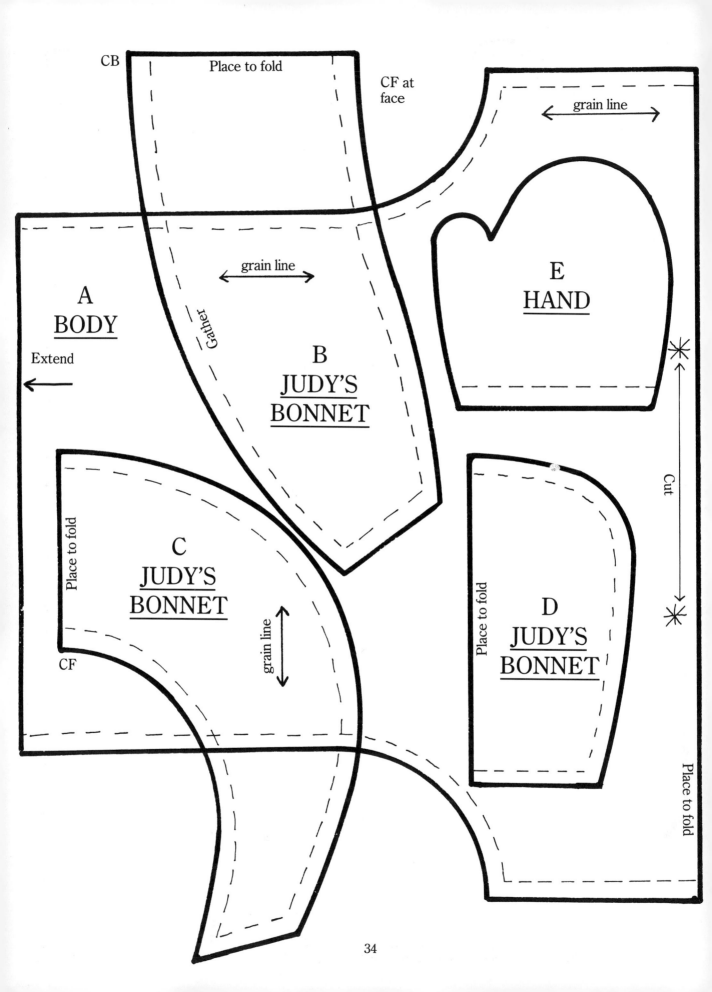

CB

Place to fold

CF at face

grain line

A
BODY

Extend

grain line

Gather

B
JUDY'S
BONNET

E
HAND

Cut

Place to fold

C
JUDY'S
BONNET

CF

grain line

Place to fold

D
JUDY'S
BONNET

Place to fold

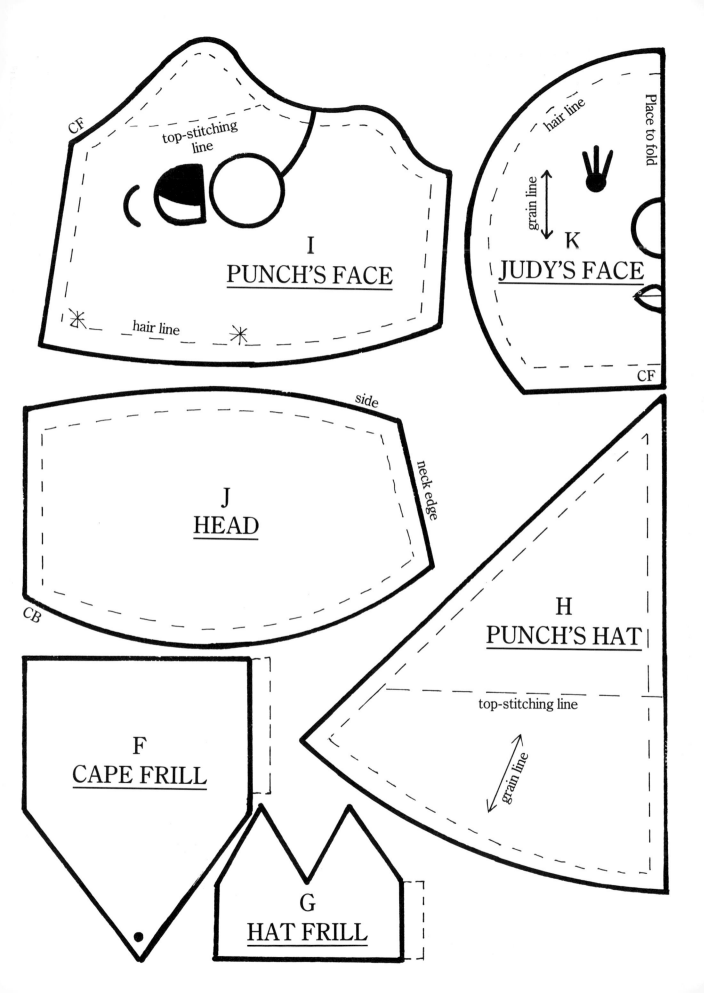

Punch's head

1 Iron interfacing to backs of face pieces.
2 Using satin stitch, embroider eyes in black and white.
3 Appliqué pink circles to cheeks.
4 Place both sides of face exactly together, RS tog, and sew centre seam.
5 Sew backs of head RS tog.
6 Sew hat front to face RS tog.
7 Sew hat back to head back RS tog.
8 Sew strands of hair in place, 6 at each side, through halfway mark of each strand.
9 Place front and back head RS tog and sew round enclosing hair in side seams. (Keep the hair out of the way by sticking Sellotape round it during sewing.)
10 Turn out through neck.
11 Top-stitch diagonal line on hat.
12 Stuff head lightly
13 Stab-stitch down the sides of the nose.
14 Embroider the mouth in stem stitch using black thread.

To attach the heads

1 Make card inserts to fit necks of suits (see pattern p 32). Push them into the heads.
2 If necessary run gathering threads round the neck edges to fit cards snugly.
3 Push a little more stuffing down into the space between card and face.
4 Glue edges of heads to card inserts.
5 Push heads into place and, tucking in SA, sew round by hand.

To finish off

1 Wrap hat trim round Punch's hat glueing overlap at CB.
2 Sew cape ends together at CB.
3 Gather up neck edge of cape and fit over Punch's head.
4 Pull up gathers and secure to neck at CB.
5 Sew 5 bells to points of cape and 1 to point of hat.
6 Tie blue ribbon round Judy's neck fastening with a bow under the chin.
7 Sew buttons on CF of dress.

Styling the hair

Punch

1 At each side make the lowest two strands of wool into curls by twisting them round a finger.
2 Sew them to the head at the side seams.
3 The back hair is drawn back and tied thus:
   i Take top strand from each side.
   ii Make a single knot at CB.
   iii Flatten the ends down.
   iv Take second strand from each side.
   v Knot them on top of the previous strands.
   vi Flatten the ends down.
   Proceed this way until all the strands are knotted in a neat row down the CB of the head.
4 Tie the remaining hair in a tight bunch with the black satin ribbon. Trim off the ends of the wool evenly, level with the neck.

Judy

Tie wool strands together at halfway mark. Fasten to face at top centre and each side. Level off at each side.

Baby (Fig 3)

An easily made baby can be held by one or other of the puppets. The face is a paper disc so any expression can be drawn on it – crying, sleeping or smiling.

1 Cut 2 circles of white card, 4cm (1½in) diam.
2 Draw the face on 1 circle with a fine black marker.
3 Cut a circle of paper lace about 2cm (¾in) larger all round than the face. Stick the lace behind the face.
4 Pad the lolly stick with a little toy filler and bind it round with bandage.
5 Sandwich one end of the stick between the 2 card circles and glue them together.
6 Tie the narrow ribbon in a bow round the baby's neck.

Fig 3
Assembling the baby

RING PUPPET

This little character could be introduced as a first string puppet. A little dexterity in the fingers is required to make him work. His hands and feet are made of Fimo *so when he is held above a hard surface he can be made to tap dance by movement of the strings. The easiest way to hold the puppet is to slip the rings over the child's fingers when the palm of the hand is facing upwards, so the rings are less liable to drop off.*

MATERIALS

A piece of white felt 15×8cm (6×3in)
3 circles of lemon yellow felt 2cm (¾in) diam
A piece of firm bright green cotton fabric
    25×50cm (10×20in)
40cm (16in) blue and white spotted ribbon 4cm (1½in)
  wide
80cm (32in) lemon satin ribbon 25mm (1in) wide
5 plastic curtain rings 25mm (1in) diam
Approx 2m (2yd) thin string or button thread in a
  neutral shade
A block of Fimo
White paint, black paint and varnish
Bright pink knitting cotton, 20 strands each 20cm (8in)
  long
Embroidery threads in lemon, pink, black and blue
White sewing thread
Green sewing thread
2 tiny beads (no larger than ½cm (¼in))
A piece of white card (postcard) 9×14cm (3½×5½in)
A small tube of silver glitter powder or glitter pen
Copydex adhesive
A handful of toy stuffing
Use of modelling tools – small knife, cocktail sticks

METHOD

1 Make pattern (see page 38). (NB There is a SA of ½cm (¼in) on the suit and the neck edge of the face only.)
2 Cut A twice in green fabric.
3 Cut C twice in white felt.
4 Cut B twice in card.
5 Transfer pattern markings to fabrics.
6 Embroider the features in satin stitch, stem stitch, French knots and daisy stitch using black and pink thread (see pages 10-11).
7 Glue the yellow felt circles to front suit at CF.
8 Apply the silver glitter to the pieces of card and allow to dry (see page 12).

37

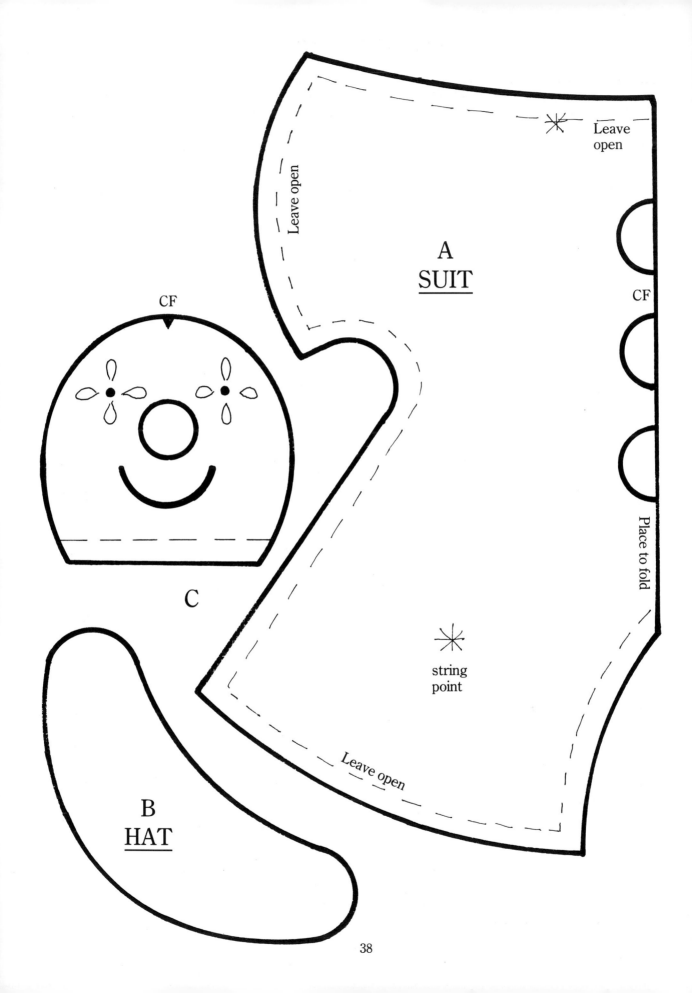

A
SUIT

Leave open

Leave open

CF

CF

Place to fold

string point

CF

C

B
HAT

Leave open

Hands and feet (see page 12 for modelling guide)
1 Divide the Fimo into 4 pieces (see Fig 1).
2 Roll the material for the hands into 2 sausage shapes.
3 Flatten these out and form the ends into flanges (Fig 2).
4 Keeping in pairs, make the thumbs by cutting a little spur at the side about halfway down.
5 Make slight indentations for the fingers and bend them inwards in a curve towards the palms.
6 Make holes through the palms using a cocktail stick.
7 Roll the material for the boots into two sausage shapes.

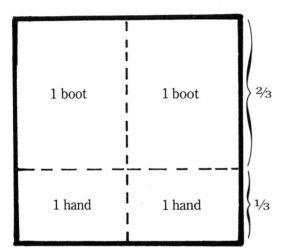

Fig 1 Division of Fimo

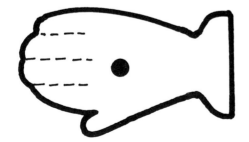

Fig 2 Hand and foot outlines

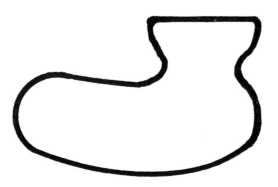

8 Bend for the ankles and make flanges (Fig 2).
9 Flatten the feet slightly at the toes and curve the feet upwards and inwards a little.
10 Bake Fimo as directed. When cool, paint the pieces white.
11 Paint black laces onto the boots (see page 12 for painting guide) and varnish each piece making sure that the holes in the hands stay open to pass the string through.

To make the doll
1 Place head pieces WS tog. Sew round leaving open at neck.
2 Stuff head and sew across opening.
3 Place suit pieces RS tog. Sew round leaving open at ankles, wrists and neck.
4 Clip SA at corners.
5 Turn out (easiest through one leg).
6 Press inside the SA at wrists and ankles.
7 Gather up these openings leaving enough room to insert hands and feet.
8 Stuff the body very lightly through neck and insert head.
9 Top-stitch across neck.
10 Insert hands and feet in place and pull up gathers tightly enclosing the flanges.
11 Make wrist and ankle frills in yellow satin ribbon (see page 15).
12 Place round wrists and ankles and pull up tight.
13 Glue both sides of the hat together at sides only.
14 Make a tassel of the pink cotton (see page 14) and sew it to the CF of the doll's head.
15 Attach the head string to the CF of the head and thread the end up through the hat.
16 Push the hat down onto the head spreading out the hair at each side with a little at the front.
17 Cut the fringe short at the front and the rest of the hair evenly.

Stringing up
1 Cut strings for the limbs about 50cm (20in) long to work with.
2 Attach leg strings at points marked with a few small stitches through the suit cloth.
3 Thread strings through the hands knotting the small beads on the undersides to anchor the strings.
4 Lay the puppet out with its head towards you and tie the ends of the strings to the rings at an even distance. (It is better to have the strings fairly short to reduce the risk of tangling.)
5 Adjust the lengths of the individual strings to fit the operator's hand and when satisfied put a dab of glue on each knot.

CONE CLOWN

This clown is in the form of the very simplest puppet. There is only one action – up and down – but the view of the doll disappearing within his own body then appearing again is very entertaining for small children. Choose the fabrics in bright, contrasting colours. The support for the puppet is a craft stick, the type used for macramé work, with a wooden knob at each end.

MATERIALS

1 wooden craft stick 28cm (11in) long
A piece of royal blue cotton fabric 28×20cm (11×8in)
A piece of bright cotton print 24cm (9½in) square (mainly red)
10cm (4in) square of white felt
10cm (4in) square of white iron-on interfacing
20cm (8in) square of strong white card
20cm (8in) square of polyester wadding
40 pieces of bright orange double-knitting cotton, each 10cm (4in) long
Embroidery threads in red, black and blue
30cm (12in) green satin ribbon 1cm (½in) wide
Copydex adhesive
Superglue or strong wood glue
A piece of flesh felt 8×15cm (3×6in)
A pinch of toy filling or cotton wool

METHOD

1 Make sure the knobs on the ends of the craft stick are secure. If not, remove them and re-apply with wood glue.
2 Make pattern (see page 42). (NB There is a SA of 1cm (½in) on piece A and 1cm (½in) at waistline of B. The other edges of B have a SA of ½cm (¼in). Piece C has a ½cm (¼in) SA all round and D has ½cm (¼in) SA at wrist edge.
3 Cut out A once in print.
4 Cut out A once, minus SA, in card.

Ring Puppet and Cone Clown

5 Cut out B twice in blue fabric.
6 Cut out C twice in flesh felt.
7 Cut out 1 pair of hands (D) in white felt and interfacing (see page 7).
8 Transfer pattern markings and features to fabrics.
9 Embroider features in satin stitch, daisy stitch and French knots using black thread for eyes and mouth and red thread for nose.
10 Sew hair in place (see page 14).

Cone

1 Glue card shape to wadding. Cut round when dry.
2 Place card, wadding side down, on WS of print leaving correct SA all round.
3 Turn in SA at base and sides and glue down onto card. Allow to dry.
4 Curl the cone shape round the craft stick and oversew the back join (see Fig 1).

Fig 1

Doll

1 Sew front head to front body RS tog at neck.
2 Sew back head to back body RS tog at neck.
3 Sew hands in place on front of suit (fold in the fingers to keep them out of the way)
4 Place front and back doll RS tog. Sew round including hair in seam and leaving suit open at base.
5 Clip SA. Turn out.
6 Push a little toy filling into the head.

Assembly

1 Push the top knob of the craft stick into the head and stitch through both sides of the neck to tighten.
2 Join bottom edge of suit to top edge of cone on seam line tucking in both SA as you go.
3 Fasten the green ribbon in a bow round the neck.
4 Catch-stitch the ribbon to the back of the neck to secure.

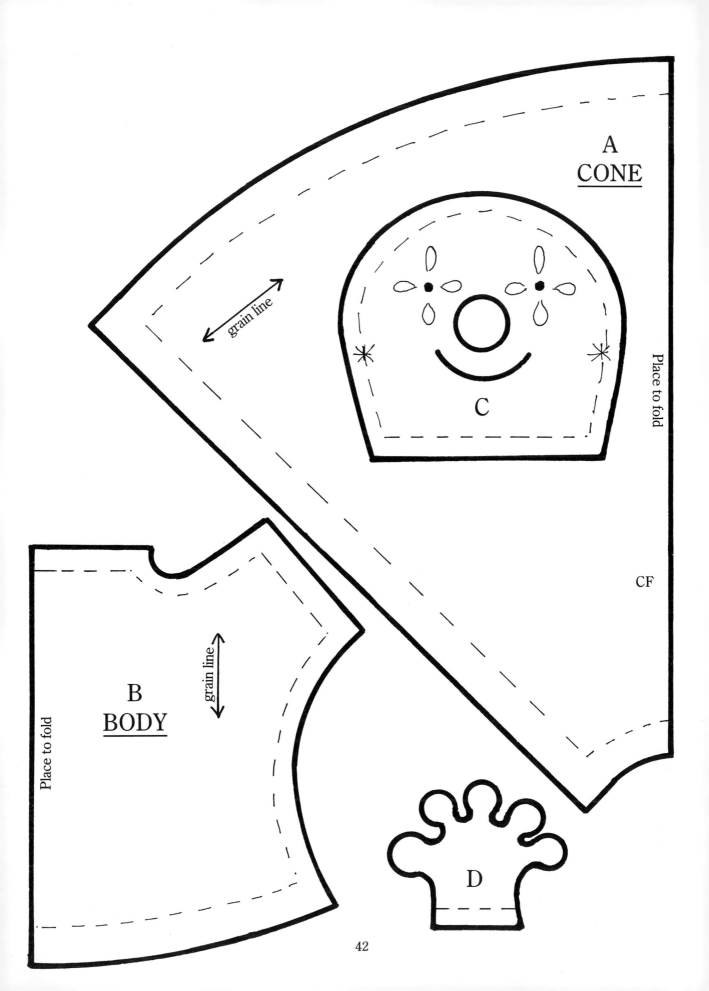

A
CONE

Place to fold

grain line

C

CF

B
BODY

Place to fold

grain line

D

42

FINGER PUPPETS

These funny little fellows are just the right size for little fingers. The basic puppet is easily constructed with a piece of card and a lightweight spun cotton ball. The 'skin' holding it all together is a piece of tubular finger bandage. There is no limit to the number of different characters you could make and the eight examples given here can be varied depending on what materials are available. The trimmings also depend on what is to hand but a bit of glitter and satin ribbon gives some sparkle. About 14cm (5½in) of ribbon will make a neck frill for one of the puppets and the amounts of felt needed are minimal.

MATERIALS

To make 8 dolls:
Approx 2m (2yd) 'tube gauze' finger
    bandage and applicator
8 pieces of white card (postcard weight),
  each 4cm (1½in) long, 5cm (2in) wide
Sellotape
Copydex adhesive
8 white spun cotton balls 25mm (1in) diam
White button thread
Assorted ribbons, felt scraps, embroidery threads,
  lace, wool etc for trimmings
Red and silver glitter
Small circles of felt punched out with an office punch

For the stage:
An empty shoe box without lid
Striped wrapping paper for covering box
60cm (24in) thin gold braid for decoration
A piece of dark material 25×30cm (10×12in)
2 double-pronged metal paper fasteners.

METHOD:

To make basic doll (see Fig 1)
1 Have pieces of Sellotape cut ready.
2 Cut bandage into lengths of 23cm (9in).
3 Roll each piece of card round a pencil to curve it.
4 Gather the bandage onto the applicator and pull off a little round the cotton ball head, thus enclosing it.

Pull off a little more bandage and wrap the card round the outside of it (i).
5 Join the card into a tube with a patch of Sellotape.
6 Push rest of bandage back over the tube and over the head again making a topknot (ii). Tie button thread round the topknot.
7 Draw features in pencil and embroider them.
  Little felt and ribbon accessories may be added with regard to the child's age.

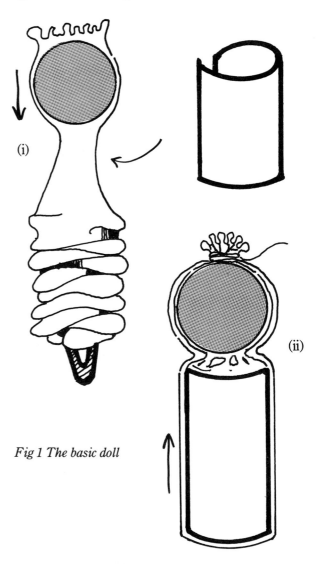

Fig 1 The basic doll

Japanese clown

Make basic puppet.

1 Make a tassel of embroidery thread at top centre of head.
2 Cut a small strip of purple felt for hair. Snip it at one edge (a). Glue to head.
3 Embroider features and stick punched out circle of pink felt at nose.
4 Tie a piece of 3mm (⅛in) ribbon tightly round neck.
5 Tint the cheeks pink with watercolour paint.

Naughtiest girl in school

Make basic puppet.

1 Cut collar (c) out of yellow felt.
2 Cut tie (d) out of blue felt and decorate with glitter stripes (see page 12).
3 Make hair with orange embroidery thread. At top leave threads about 5cm (2in) long and tie together with a piece of 3mm (⅛in) ribbon. Make knotted tufts at each side of head.
4 Embroider features and stick red felt nose in place.
5 Stick tie in place under chin with a dab of glue.
6 Wrap collar round doll's neck and fasten with small stitches.

Sailor clown

Make basic puppet.

1 Cut out hat (b) twice in white felt. Sew round outside close to edge.
2 Place on head over topknot and fasten with small stitches at each side.
3 Make hair with loops of red embroidery thread at each side.
4 Make neck frill from royal blue satin ribbon 1cm (½in) wide×14cm (5½in) long.
5 Stick red punched-out nose on face and embroider features.

Fez

Make basic puppet.

1 Cut shape (k) twice in red felt. Sew the pieces together and make a few loops of black thread at the top.
2 Punch out 4 circles of red felt and stick 1 on the doll's face for a nose and the other 3 at CF of body.
3 Make a ribbon frill from turquoise satin ribbon 1cm (½in) wide and apply tightly round the doll's neck.
4 Embroider features in black thread.
5 Place hat on doll's head and fix with small stitches at each side.

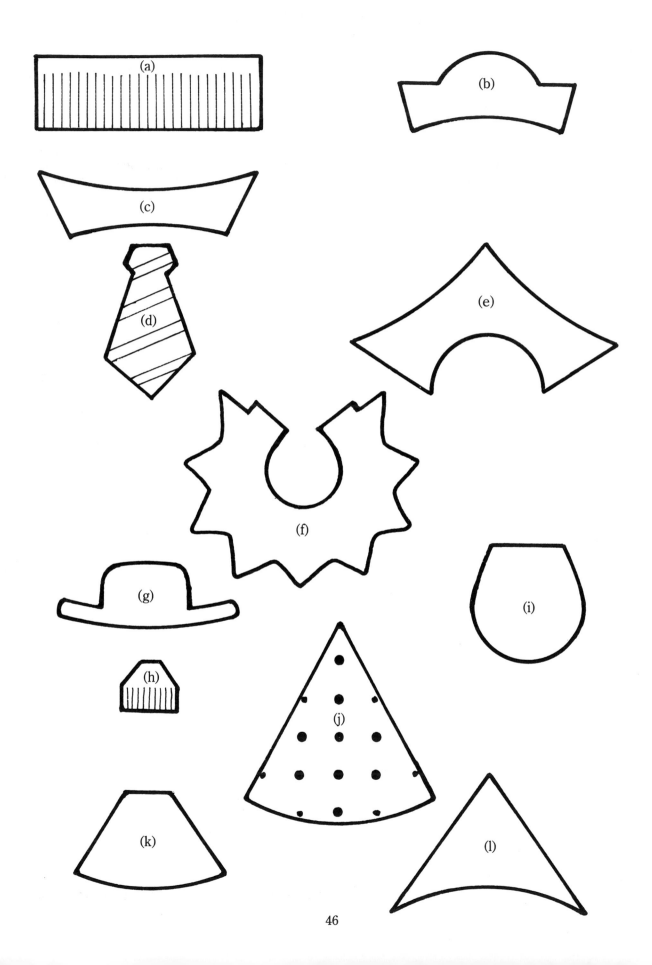

Jester

Make basic puppet.
1 Cut shape (e) twice in blue felt.
2 Cut shape (f) once in green and outline the edge with glitter (see page 12).
3 Stick red circle felt nose in place and embroider features in black.
4 Sew both sides of hat together and make thread loops at the three points with yellow thread.
5 Fasten cape round neck and fix with a few stitches at CB.
6 Put hat on doll's head and fasten with stitches at each side.

Lacey

Make basic puppet.
1 Cut shape (l) twice in yellow felt.
2 Make 3 loops of narrow ribbon and enclose them at the point of the hat when sewing together.
3 Punch out 4 circles of pink felt and stick 1 to the doll's face for a nose and the other 3 at CF of suit.
4 Make a neck frill from some dainty lace 1cm (½in) wide and apply it tightly round the doll's neck.
5 Embroider features in black thread.
6 Place hat on doll's head and fasten with small stitches at each side.
7 Make loops with orange thread at each side of head.

Moustache clown

Make basic puppet.
1 Cut shape (g) twice in black felt and moustache (h) once.
2 Stick red felt nose on face with moustache underneath it. Embroider features.
3 Sew 2 sides of hat together and fasten to head with small stitches at each side.
4 With brown thread make loops at each side of head.
5 Cut dicky shape (i) out of white felt and attach round doll's neck with a few stitches at CB.
6 Paint glitter dots (see page 12) on a piece of satin ribbon 1cm (½in) wide and tie in a bow round neck.

Wizard clown

Make basic puppet.
1 Stick red felt nose in place and embroider features in black.
2 Cut shape (j) twice in orange felt and dot the surfaces with silver glitter.
3 Sew both pieces together and fasten to doll's head with small stitches at each side.
4 Make loops at each side of head with green embroidery thread.
5 Tie a bow round neck with orange satin ribbon 1cm (½in) wide.

Stage

1 Cover an empty shoe box with patterned wrapping paper.
2 Make a template using shape (m) (below). This is the area that must be cut out of the card to form a stage.
3 On the bottom of the box, position the template at one end equidistant from the edges. Draw round it and then with a sharp knife or scissors cut away the opening.
4 Glue the thin gold braid to the outside of the box at the cut edge.
5 Make the background curtain from the dark material. At one end make a turning of 1cm (½in). At the opposite end make a narrow hem. Pass about 30cm (12in) of thread through the top turning.
6 Push the pronged paper fasteners through the cardboard sides at the top of the box and string the curtain across by winding the ends of the thread tightly round them. The material will be slightly gathered so the puppeteer's hand can pass in front of the curtain.

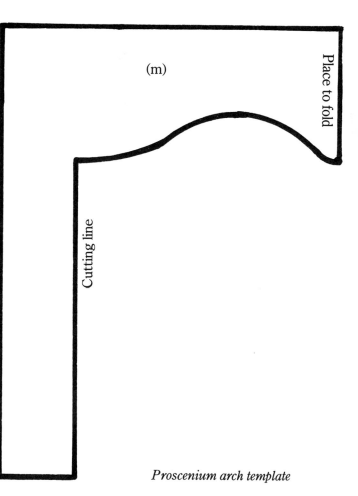

(m)

Place to fold

Cutting line

Proscenium arch template

STRIPEY DOLL

 This jolly stripey clown is suitable for the older child or teenager. A younger child would want him to have removable clothes and he is constructed all in one. Also, materials like satin and velvet are difficult to clean and make this design impractical for the nursery. The doll stands about 50cm (20in) high.

MATERIALS

A piece of blue velvet 76cm (30in) wide×
   15cm (6in) long
Red and white striped polycotton 92cm
   (36in) wide×41cm (16in) long (stripes
running lengthways)
Flesh-coloured double stockinette 26cm (10in) wide×
   31cm (12in) long
18cm (7in) square iron-on interfacing
2 circles of black felt 2cm (¾in) diam
2 circles of white felt 2cm (¾in) diam
Approx 8m (8yd) bright yellow double-knitting wool
A piece of red satin 54cm (21in) wide×64cm (25in) long
23cm (9in) square of white polycotton
A piece of white organdie 63×37cm (25×14½in)
3m (3yd) of red satin bias binding 2cm (¾in) wide
Approx 400g (14oz) toy filling
2 flat white buttons 25mm (1in) diam
Black embroidery thread
Flesh pink embroidery thread
Sewing threads in red, white and blue

METHOD

1 Make pattern (see pages 50-1). (NB There
   is a SA of 1cm (½in) on all pieces except
   hat section, brim edge of hat and all boot
   edges except top of boot. These have a
SA of ½cm (¼in). When cutting the fabric remember
that satin, velvet and stockinette are all one-way
fabrics. So is a vertical stripe on the trousers.)
2 Transfer markings to fabrics.
3 Cut out A once in blue velvet with CF to fold.

4 Cut out A once again with back extension of 1cm
   (½in).
5 Cut out B once and C twice in double stockinette.
6 Cut out D twice in double stockinette.
7 Cut E twice on folded white polycotton.
8 Cut F 6 times in red satin.
9 Cut G 4 times in red satin (2 pairs).
10 Cut H twice in red satin.
11 Cut I 4 times (2 pairs) in red satin.
12 For the trousers, cut 2 pieces in red and white
   stripe, each 46cm (18in) wide×33cm (13in) long.
   (The remainder makes a waistband 8×33cm (3×
   13in).)
13 Using white organdie, cut 1 neck frill 9×63cm
   (3½×25in); cut 2 wrist frills 6×42cm (2½×17in);
   cut 2 ankle frills 8×53cm (3×21in).
14 Cut red satin bias into lengths to fit frill edges.

Hat

1 Back the underbrim pieces with interfacing.
2 Sew the 6 crown pieces RS tog to meet at top
   centre.
3 Sew brim pieces RS tog at side seams.
4 Sew underbrim pieces RS tog at side seams.
5 Place brim and underbrim RS tog and sew round
   perimeter seam.
6 Turn out and press lightly.
7 Sew round brim at head seam.
8 Top-stitch round brim edge ½cm (¼in) from edge
   (Fig 1).
9 Place brim over hat crown, RS tog.
10 Sew round head seam.

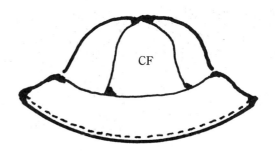

Fig 1 Top-stitching round brim

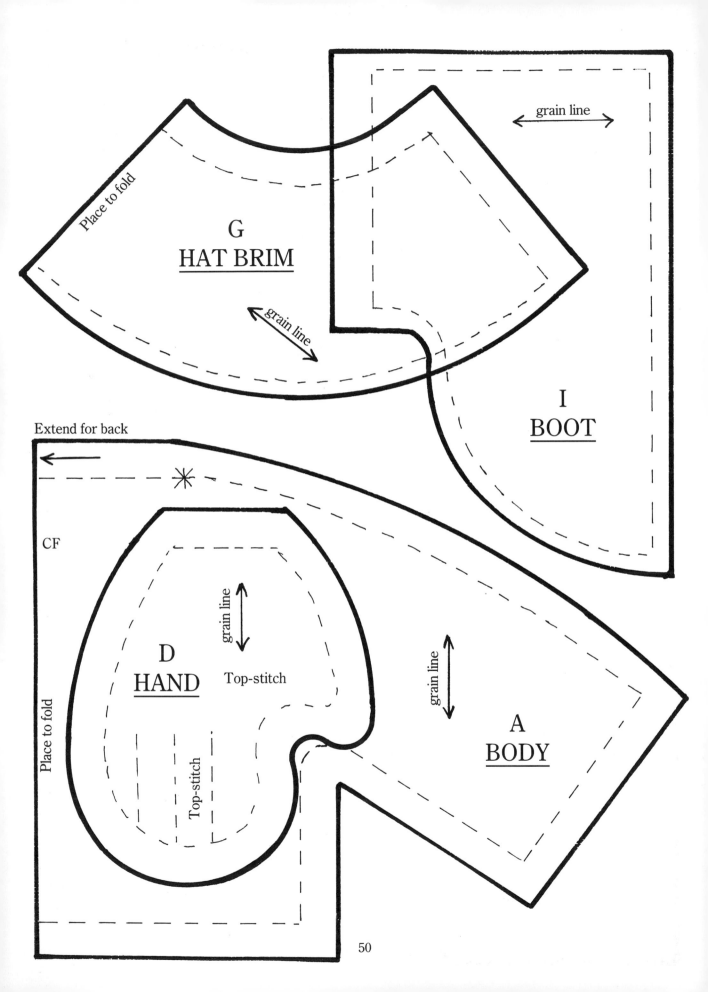

G
HAT BRIM

Place to fold

grain line

grain line

I
BOOT

Extend for back

CF

*

Place to fold

D
HAND

grain line

Top-stitch

Top-stitch

grain line

A
BODY

50

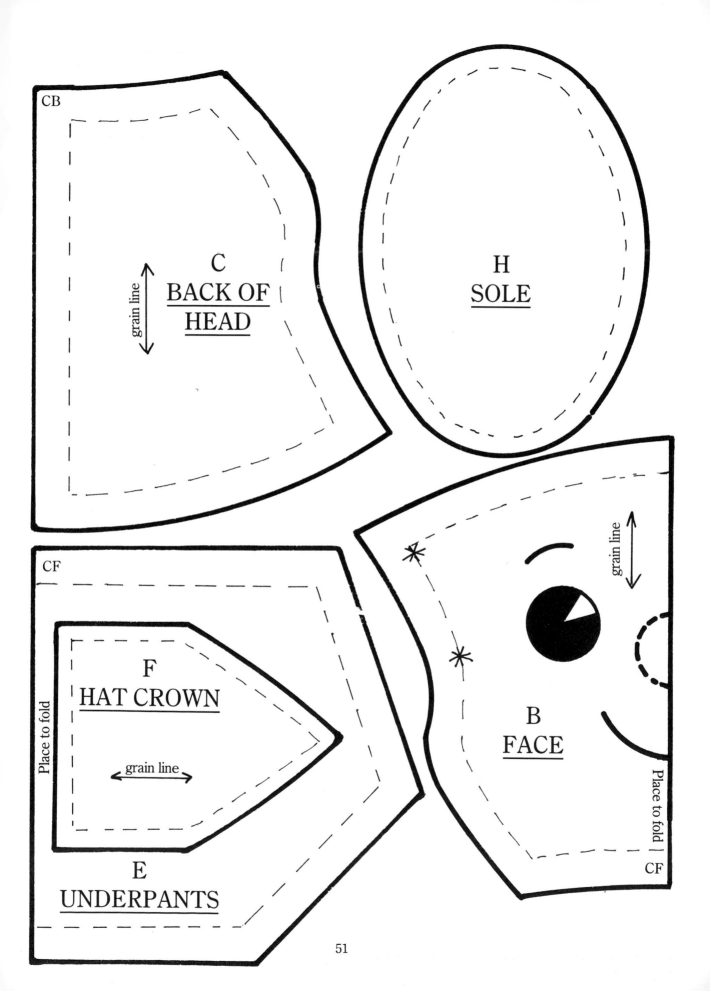

CB

C
grain line
BACK OF
HEAD

H
SOLE

CF

F
HAT CROWN

grain line

Place to fold

E
UNDERPANTS

B
FACE

grain line

Place to fold

CF

51

Face

1 Make patent nose on face (see page 13).
2 Mark eye and mouth positions on front of face.
3 Make pie-slice eyes (see page 13).
4 Appliqué eyes to face. Embroider mouth and eyebrows in stem stitch with black thread.
5 Stay-stitch round 3 head pieces.

Hair

Cut yellow wool into 32 strands (16 for each side), each strand 24cm (9½in) long. Sew to front of face at places marked.

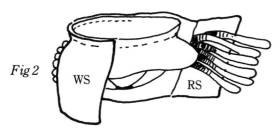

Fig 2

Head

1 Sew back of head pieces to face RS tog at sides, including hair in seams.
2 Pin face round hat RS tog and sew round head seam leaving SA free (Fig 2).
3 Tucking in SA oversew CB seam for about 6cm (2½in).

Ankle frills

1 Apply satin bias to one edge of each strip.
2 Join the ends with a French seam.
3 Gather up organdie to fit boot tops.

Wrist frills

1 Apply satin bias to one edge of each strip.
2 Join the ends with a French seam (see page 16).
3 Gather up organdie to fit wrist edge of sleeve.

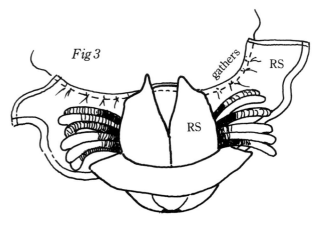

Fig 3

Neck frill

1 Apply satin bias to one edge of organdie strip.
2 Make a narrow hem at each end.
3 Gather up organdie to fit neck edge of head (Fig 3).

Hands

Use single stockinette.
1 Sew round in pairs leaving open at wrists.
2 Clip SA. Turn out and stuff lightly.
3 Close off opening.
4 Top-stitch down finger lines through thickness of hand (Fig 4).

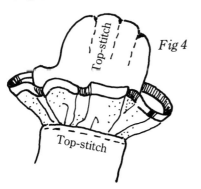

Fig 4

Body

1 Place pieces RS tog. Sew shoulder seams.
2 Sew underarm seams.
3 Clip SA. Turn out. Press SA on sleeve ends to inside.
4 Tack wrist frills over hands and insert hands into sleeve openings.
5 Top-stitch across wrists through all layers (Fig 4).

Underpants

Place two sides of underpants RS tog. Sew all round except for waist opening. (No leg openings needed.)

To join up

1 Place neck frill over neck edge of head RS tog with opening at CB. Leave SA at back of head free. Sew round neck seam (Fig 3).
2 Place body over neck edge with RS of velvet against underside of frill, matching up back openings. Sew round neck seam again.
3 With RS tog, join CB seam of body for 6cm (2½in) up from waist (Fig 5). Leave rest of seam open.
4 With RS tog, join underpants to body at waist.
5 Clip corners and turn out.
6 Stuff the doll through this back opening fairly tightly, starting with the arms first, then hat and head and finally the rest of the body.
7 Close up the back opening by hand tucking in SA and changing thread colour when necessary.

The bottom half of the doll is made separately.
1 Make boots (see page 16).
2 Place ankle frills over boot tops. Sew through all layers with seam going front to back.

Trousers

1 Fold each piece of trouser material in half length-ways, RS tog, and mark 15cm (6in) down from waistline. The rest is inside leg seam.
2 Sew each inside leg.
3 Turn one leg out. Slip other leg inside so legs are RS tog.
4 Sew round crotch seam from front to back leaving last 8cm (3in) open at CB.
5 Gather round waist edge and apply waistband (Fig 5).
6 Gather ankle edges to fit over tops of boots.
7 Push boots into ankle openings, toes pointing forwards, and sew across inside.
8 Stuff trouser legs loosely and pull trousers over body.
9 Handsew trousers to body on the waistline seam catching reverse of waistband to clown's body with firm stitches.
10 Oversew gap in CB seam of trousers.
11 Sew two white buttons on waistband front. (Catch the two sides of the neck frill together with a few small stitches just above bias binding.)

Fig 5

BABY CLOWN

This little doll is small enough to be handled comfortably. The head is made from a sponge ball enclosed by a piece cut from a discarded nylon stocking and, as the quantities of materials required are small, the whole doll can be made with scraps of wool and cloth left over from other projects.

The doll's head is not complicated by ears so the neck frill folds upwards to disguise the fact.

If a second ball is not available for the body an extra handful of toy stuffing can be used instead.

MATERIALS

2 soft yellow sponge balls 23cm (9in) circumference
1 white or flesh-coloured nylon stocking
15cm (6in) square white felt
12cm (5in) orange polycotton 114cm (45in) wide
Orange and white windowpane check cotton fabric 92cm (36in) wide×35cm (14in) long
3 bright pink pompons 25mm (1in) diam
30 pieces of blue chunky wool, each 30cm (12in) long
Scrap of black felt
Scrap of pink felt
2 handfuls of toy stuffing
Copydex adhesive
Flesh-coloured embroidery thread
Black embroidery thread
Sewing thread in orange, pink and white

METHOD

1 Make pattern (opposite). (NB The SA on the frills and the suit is 1cm (½in). The SA on the wrist edge of hand and ankle edge of boot is 1cm (½in). SA on the rest of boots is ½cm (¼in). No SA on curve of hand.)
2 Cut out A twice from check cotton fabric.
3 Cut out 4 frills, 25×10cm (10×4in), from same.
4 Cut out B 4 times from plain orange cotton and 2 boot soles C from same.

5 Cut an orange neck frill 12×50cm (5×20in).
6 Cut D 4 times from white felt.
7 Cut a piece of stocking from narrowest part of leg 25cm (10in) long.

Hair and head

1 Make a tassel using the blue wool (see page 14).
2 Cut out the top of one sponge ball to fit the knob of the tassel. Save the cut out bit for the nose.
3 Push the sponge ball into the piece of stocking with the hollow at the top.
4 Fold in the raw edge of the stocking and run a gathering thread round.
5 Push the end of the tassel into the hollow in the ball and tighten the gathering thread to enclose the tassel. Knot the thread and dab the knot with glue.
6 Push the sponge piece cut from the ball up into place behind the stocking in the centre of the intended face. Sew round it with running stitches and pull up slightly to form a protruding nose.
7 Push two evenly matched pinches of toy filling into the doll's cheeks and one pinch into the chin.
8 Run a gathering thread round the neck and pull up tight.

Hands

Join hands together in pairs. Sew close to the edge and leave the wrists open. Stuff lightly and close edge.

Boots

Make boots following method on page 16.

Frills

1 Make double-folded frills (see page 15), 1 plain orange neck frill and 4 in check fabric.
2 Pull up gathers to fit neck, arm and leg openings.
3 Place the check frills over the tops of boots and hands and sew across on seam line.

Suit

1 Sew the pompons on at CF.
2 Place back and front suit pieces RS tog. Sew seams at sides, two short shoulder seams and two short inside leg seams. Leave open at neck, arm, leg and base of suit.

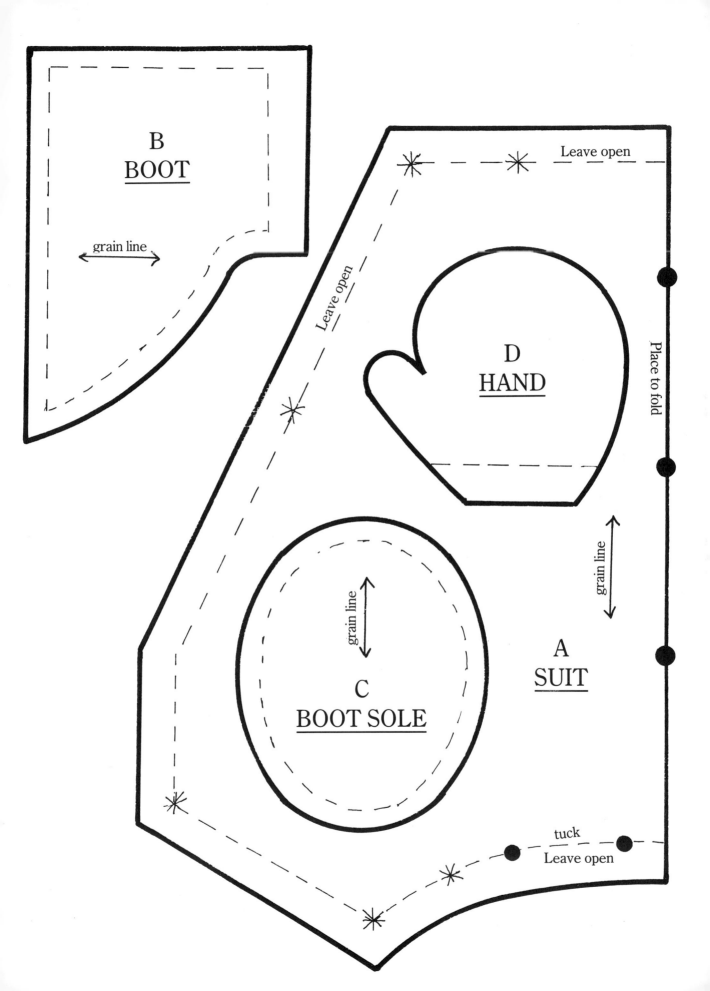

3 Push into place, through the inside of the suit; the arms (with thumbs pointing up) and the feet (with toes pointing outwards). Sew across on seam lines.

4 Make small pleats in suit opening at back and front. Sew them down for about 2cm (¾in).

To join head to body

1 Pull up the gathers in the neck frill to fit the neck of the suit.

2 Pass the unstuffed end of the stocking through the neck frill and sew across with the pleats of the frill up round the head.

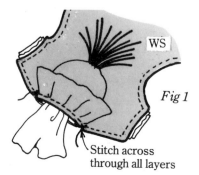

WS

Fig 1

Stitch across
through all layers

3 Still keeping suit inside out, push the head of the doll into place (facing front). Pull the end of the stocking through the neck opening. Sew across through all layers (see Fig 1).

4 Push the second ball, or a handful of toy filling, into the stocking. Push well in and make a knot in the end of the stocking. Trim excess below knot.

5 Turn out the doll by grasping the head and pulling it out of the opening at the base of the suit.

6 Add more toy filling to the body.

7 Close the opening by oversewing and tucking in the SA at the same time.

To finish

1 For the mouth, cut half a small circle from pink felt and glue in place.

2 Cut 2 eyes from black felt. Stick them in place. Alternatively, embroider the features.

3 Embroider eyebrows and eyelashes to suit face and, if desired, dab on spots of white paint to enhance the eyes. Tint the doll's cheeks with a little red watercolour.

4 Trim the doll's hair so it falls level with the eyes.

PUFF-BALL DOLL

This bright little clown is suitable for hanging in prams. Beads and net puffs are strung in such a way that all the cords are tied together in a central knot on top of the head and covered with a felt hat. There are no raw fabric edges.

MATERIALS

Natural wood macramé beads with large holes:

    1 large barrel bead 6cm (2½in) long (body)

1 round bead 3cm (1¼in) diam (head)

4 round beads 25mm (1in) diam (hands and feet)

4 round, red beads 1cm (½in) diam (stops)

Approx 37m (40yd) bright red knitting cotton

2 red round stickers 8mm (⅜in) diam

Black and white fine marker pens

Copydex adhesive

High-gloss varnish

Fine glasspaper

Plasticine and golf tees to support beads during painting

1m (1yd) bright green stiff nylon net 92cm (36in) wide

10cm (4in) square of yellow felt

3 small circles of purple felt 5mm (¼in) diam

8cm (3in) square of white felt

8cm (3in) square of iron-on interfacing

Bright green embroidery thread

Yellow embroidery thread

White crayon pencil for marking out net circles

25cm (10in) double-sided red satin ribbon 1cm (½in) wide

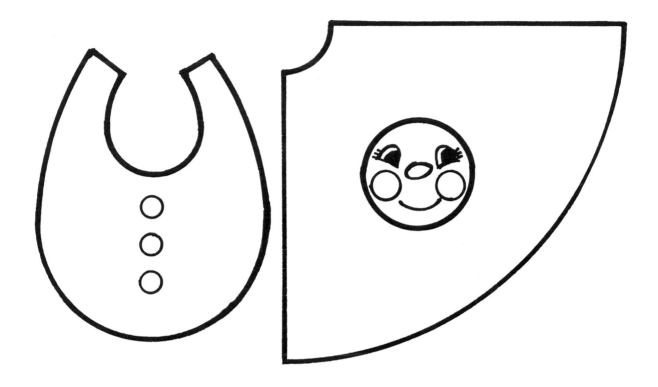

METHOD

To make net circles

1 Cut net up into 15cm (6in) squares. You will need 36.

2 Using round templates or a set of compasses mark the net into circles. (Several layers can be cut at once.)

3 Cut 20 circles (10 for each leg) 13cm (5in) diam.

4 Cut 16 circles (8 for each arm) 10cm (4in) diam.

5 Make into puffs (see page 15).

To make head

1 If the bead is varnished it won't take the decoration so remove the varnish first by sanding.

2 Copy the features onto the face of the bead. Stick the cheeks in place (see page 13).

3 Give the head 2 coats of varnish.

Hat

1 Copy hat shape onto yellow felt once and cut out.

2 Sew up back seam close to the edge leaving hole at top point. Turn back the brim about 1cm (½in).

Dicky (Bib)

Cut dicky shape out of white felt and stick purple felt circles at CF.

To join up

1 Cut small slits in the undersides of the puffs at the centres.

2 Lay out the beads and puffs in the order they will be used (see Fig 1).

3 Cut red knitting cotton into lengths of about 90cm (1yd) long. You need 40 for 1 doll.

To assist with threading thick amounts of yarn use a piece of yarn to pull the rest through (see page 7). Take care not to tear the net when threading the puffs.

Legs and arms

1 Thread 5 strands of red cotton through each leg stop bead.

2 Pull the bead halfway down and clump the threads together.

3 Pull the 10 strands through each foot bead.

4 Pull the 10 strands through 10 puffs for each leg.

5 Join the strands from each leg together and pass all 20 through the body bead.

Make the arms in the same way as the legs but with 8 puffs each.

Top knot

You now have to thread all 40 strands through the head bead.

1 At the top of the head bead divide the strands into 2 equal bunches and tie them together in a big double knot. Dab the knot with glue to secure.

2 Make 2 plaits of 3 strands each taken from the main bunch. Let the rest of the red cotton fall back over the doll's head.

To finish off

1 Push the cone hat onto the doll's head and bring the 2 plaited cords out through the hole in the point.

2 Tie the cords together with a weaver's knot (see page 9) to form the hanging loop. A few stitches through the point of the hat into the cords will stop the hat riding up.

3 Trim the hair evenly round the doll's face.

4 Fix the dicky to the doll's front with a few stitches at the back neck.

5 Tie the red satin ribbon in a bow round the neck.

6 Catch-stitch the ribbon to the dicky at CB of doll's neck.

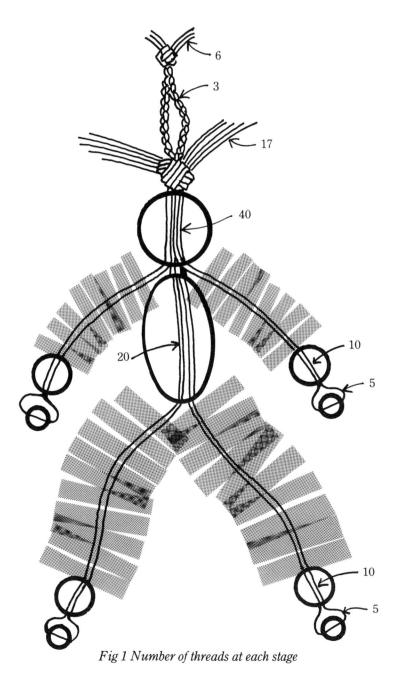

Fig 1 Number of threads at each stage

DRESSING-TABLE DOLL

It is now virtually impossible to find those little china ladies in lavender-filled crinolines that used to loll about on dressing-table tops during the Twenties and Thirties, so why not make your own? This version is in the form of a Venetian, white-faced clown in a spangled suit. Rose potpourri or lavender seeds may be used for the filling. The 'china' parts of the doll are made from Fimo, a ceramic substitute, or other craft clay, which does not need firing to harden. Those readers who are experienced potters may prefer to make the hard parts of the doll in clay with conventional firing and glazing but remember that, unlike Fimo, clay shrinks on firing, so you must adjust the proportions of material accordingly. The finished doll stands 25cm (10in) high.

MATERIALS

1 block of transparent Fimo
A piece of turquoise satin 46cm (18in) wide, 23cm (9in) long
35cm (14in) pink satin ribbon 1cm (½in) wide
24 pink sequins
25g (1oz) potpourri or lavender filling
A small handful of toy filling
Embroidery threads in cream and turquoise
50cm (20in) cream lace 5cm (2in) wide
20cm (8in) cream lace 3cm (1in) wide
Matt white paint
Matt black paint
Clear varnish
Black fine marker pen
Pink fine marker pen
Plasticine to support pieces during painting
A small sharp knife
Cocktail sticks
Baking tray
Plate for modelling on
Copydex adhesive

METHOD

Divide Fimo into sections as shown in Fig 1. (See instructions for modelling, page 12.)

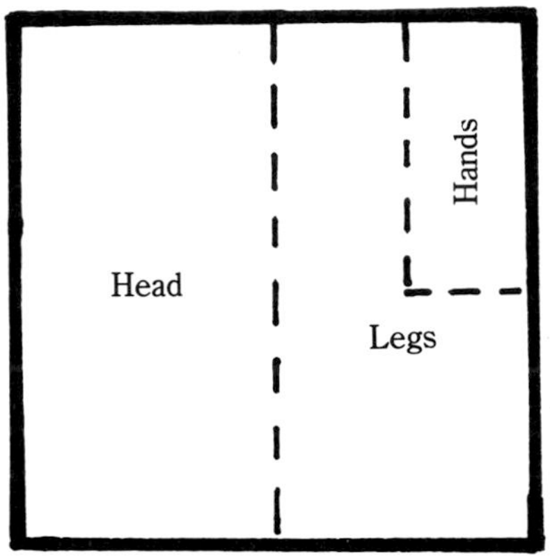

Fig 1 Division of Fimo

[Diagram showing a square divided into sections labelled: Head, Hands, Legs]

Head

1 Make a sausage shape 6cm (2½in) long.
2 Indent the neck about one third from one end. Form the shape of the head above this. Don't make the neck too thin. (One half of a cocktail stick can be pushed up through the base of the neck into the head to give it strength.)
3 Press out the base to form a flange which will later support the fabric of the suit.
4 Make sure that the head is evenly balanced – there is as much of the head at the back of the neck as at the front. Keep modelling until a pleasant shape is obtained with a rather sad expression on the face and a long straight nose. This may take a long time depending on your skill as a sculptor. Check the shape from all angles by turning the plate round (Fig 2, p62).
5 Place the finished piece on the baking tray.

Hands

1 Divide the portion of Fimo for the hands into 2 equal parts and mould them into lozenge shapes.
2 Treating the hands as a pair, cut a spur for each thumb. With the knife mark the fingers without going through the thickness of the hand, then curl the fingers towards the palms slightly (Fig 2, p62).
3 Place the hands on the tray beside the head.

Legs

1 Divide portion of Fimo set aside for the legs into 2 equal parts.
2 Roll each into a sausage shape 8cm (3in) long.
3 About one third from the end of each one bend a foot at right angles and make a heel. Flatten the sole slightly and taper the ankle. Turn the toes in a little to make a pair and make flanges and grooves at the leg tops (Fig 2, p62). Place the legs on the tray beside the head and hands.

Harden the Fimo according to the manufacturer's instructions.

When the pieces are cooled paint and varnish them (see pages 12-13).

Body

1 Make a pattern for the suit (see page 62). (A ½cm (¼in) SA is allowed.)
2 Transfer pattern to fabric and cut 2.
3 Cut into fabric at sleeve and crotch where marked.
4 Place back to front RS tog and sew round leaving open at wrists, neck and legs.
5 Clip SA at corners and turn suit out through neck opening.
6 Press the SA on the leg openings to the inside.

Assembly

1 Gather round leg openings and insert leg flanges. Pull gathers tight and secure thread carefully.
2 Glue the wrist part of the hands and insert them into the openings in the suit. Pinch the fabric while it dries to the hands.
3 Cut the narrower lace into 2 equal parts and gather them up to fit each wrist. Fasten lace over raw edge of satin so that it falls in folds over the hand.
4 Using a large funnel, fill the body with potpourri, leaving the top half and the sleeves empty.
5 Push toy filler evenly into both sleeves and the top part of the body.
6 Insert the doll's head at the neck and oversew the opening at each side keeping the chin central.
7 Make a neck frill from the wider lace. Gather one edge and slip the frill over the doll's head. Pull up the gathers tightly. Finish off at the back.
8 Tie the pink satin ribbon in a bow round the neck above the lace frill.
9 Decorate the suit with pink sequins. The easiest way to apply sequins is to glue them to the fabric. Dab the glue onto the satin first, a tiny dot on the end of a cocktail stick will suffice. Pick up a sequin with a wetted finger and pop it onto the glue before it dries. Don't overload the suit with sequins but just add a few to the outer edge of each thigh.

DRESSING-TABLE DOLL

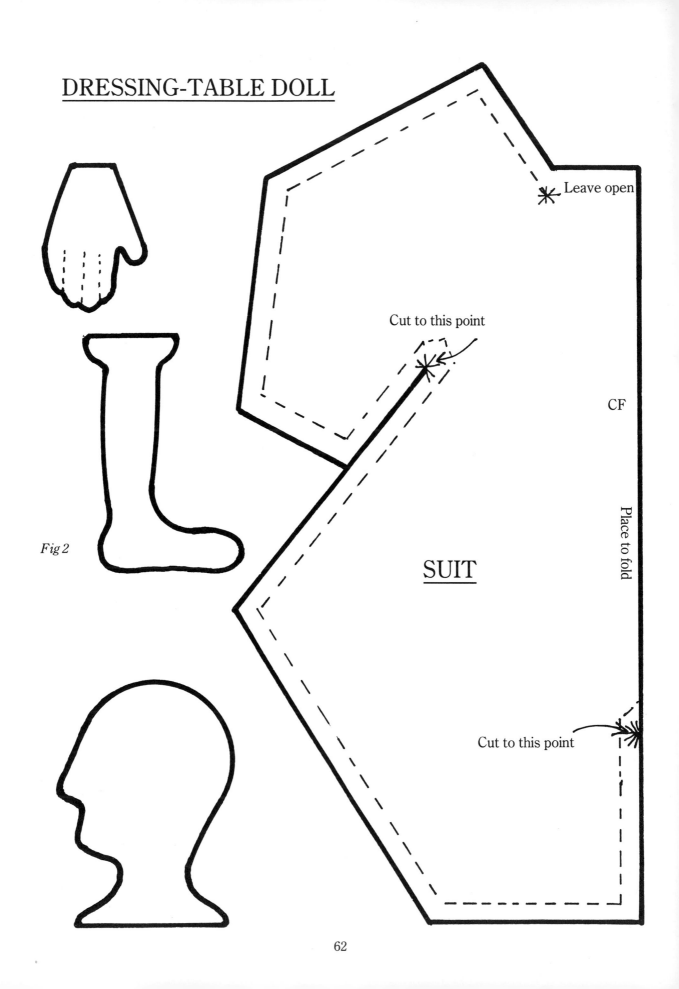

Fig 2

Leave open

Cut to this point

CF

Place to fold

SUIT

Cut to this point

HARLEQUIN QUILT

This beautiful quilt would make a splendid cover for a teenage girl's divan. The quilt top consists of many diamond-shaped patches of satin machined together in the manner of a harlequin's suit. A clown face motif with a loose net frill is attached to one corner of the quilt. A further extension of the design would be to make a large cushion in one of the satins used on the quilt, on the front of which could be sewn a second, matching clown's face.

If the cost of satin is prohibitive, an equally attractive but less luxurious version can be made using plain cottons in well chosen combinations of colour. A cotton topped quilt has the added advantage of being washable (on lowest machine code) whereas the satin one will need dry-cleaning. Both types of quilt are backed with cotton sheeting to stop them sliding off the bed. The material used in the sample is heavy, acetate satin which can be easily torn into strips without spoiling. Cotton sheeting can similarly be 'ripped up' thus saving time when cutting out the patches.

Keep in mind that satin is a one-way fabric so be alert when cutting out and making up the quilt top.

MATERIALS

Heavy, high lustre satins 112cm (44/45in) wide:
  3m (3½yd) background colour (cream)
  1m (1yd) each of peach, green, blue and gold satin
6m (6yd) polyester wadding (Batting) 92cm (36in) wide
280cm (3yd) plain cotton sheeting 178cm (70in) wide
11m (11yd) satin border ribbon, already folded

For the decoration
1m (1¼yd) white stiff net 114cm (45in) wide
A piece of white satin 28cm (11in) square
A piece of black satin 28cm (11in) square
A piece of iron-on interfacing 36cm (14in) square
Polyester wadding 38cm (15in) square
White muslin 38cm (15in) square
2 black felt circles 2cm (¾in) diam
A piece of pink felt 13cm (5in) square
Black sewing thread
Pink sewing thread
A large bobbin of machine thread in cream or neutral
Pink buttonhole thread for tying the quilt layers
Sequins (optional)
Copydex adhesive
3 pieces of fairly stiff card A3 size
Ruler, set-square, string and chalk

METHOD

Preparation

Make cardboard templates in the shapes shown (see Fig 1). To construct a diamond 40cm (16in) tall × 23cm (9in) wide:

1 Take 1 piece of card at least 40cm × 23cm (16 × 9in).
2 Mark halfway points along each side and join them with a horizontal and a vertical line. They form right angles at the centre point.
3 At each side of the centre point mark off 11.5cm (4½in) along the horizontal.
4 At each side of the centre point mark off 20cm (8in) on the vertical.
5 Join these points into a diamond. Cut out the shape and use this as a master.
6 On a second piece of card draw round the master diamond and cut this one out. Use this as the whole diamond template.
7 Draw another diamond on the third piece of card. Cut it out and cut it in half horizontally. This is the 'short half'.
8 Cut one of the triangles – a short half – in half again vertically to form the quarter shape.
9 To make the 'long half' cut the master diamond in half vertically.

These templates can be used to cut out all the patches needed for the quilt. (NB They have no SA included so add 1cm (½in) all round when cutting out.)

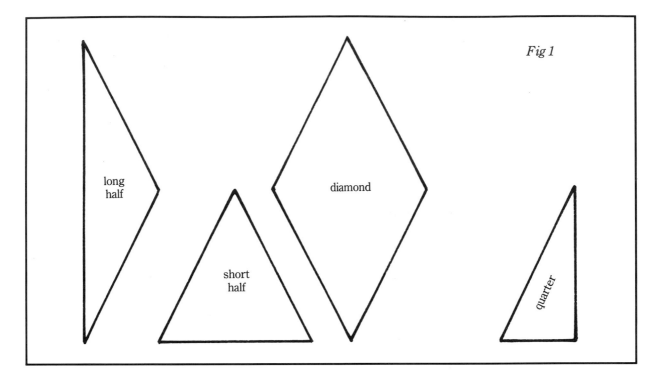

Fig 1

Cutting out

You will need 42 coloured patches, all full diamonds. A suggested division is 10 each of blue and green and 11 each of peach and gold. The cream background patches are as follows:

(i)   4 quarters, cut in 2 pairs, for the corners
(ii) 10 long halves
(iii) 12 short halves
(iv) 30 full diamonds

To tear the fabric across the grain measure the required distance down the selvedge and make a little straight cut. Be bold and rip the material straight across. Snip the other selvedge with scissors.

Background patches

1 For full diamonds tear the cream satin into 11 strips, each 22cm (9in) deep.

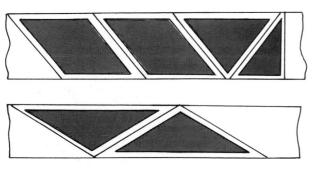

Fig 2 Templates and cutting out

2 Laying the diamond template on its side, and leaving the correct amount of SA all round, cut the strip into patches (see Fig 2). You will get 3 full diamonds out of each strip plus 1 short half. The remaining short halves and the 4 quarters can be cut out of the eleventh strip.

3 For the 10 long halves, tear 4 strips of satin, each 13.50cm (5½in) deep from the remaining fabric.

Assorted colour patches

1 Tear 4 strips of each colour 22cms (9in) deep.

2 Cut out the whole diamonds as before.

Unavoidably there will be satin left over but it is better to have some leeway in case of bad cutting. The wastage has been kept to a minimum.

To make up the quilt top

1 With a soft pencil lightly mark the sewing lines on the reverse of the patches. Use the templates to draw round.

2 Following Fig 3, sew the patches together in diagonal strips, starting at what will be the top left-hand corner of the quilt. Use good machine thread in cream or neutral and be exact on the SA of every patch. Each coloured patch is always separated from another by a background patch.

3 When all the strips are done start to sew the strips RS tog. Pin first, to check that the seams meet at the correct points without too much trouble. Don't open out the SA on the patches and strips but fold

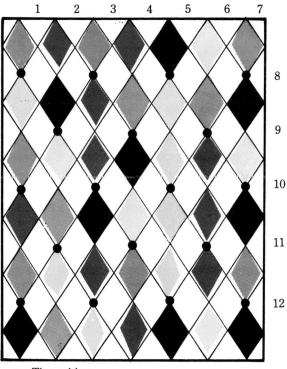

1 2 3 4 5 6 7

8

9

10

11

12

● = Tie positions

Fig 3 Making up quilt top

them over in one direction. This prevents seams pulling apart when the quilt is in use.

4 Measure the quilt top when it is finished. It should be approximately 161×240cm (63×96in).

To join up

Have the backing sheet and the wadding at least 8cm (3in) bigger all round than the quilt top as they have to extend beyond the edge of the top quilt. You will have to 'cut and butt' the wadding into a piece the required area (see page 7, sewing information). For example, if the wadding is 92cm (36in) wide you will need 3 lengths of 2m (2yd) each joined together with the joins going horizontally across the quilt. Don't overlap the joins as this will cause ridges. Butt the edges of the wadding and oversew them roughly and loosely using a length of thin wool and a large needle. As the quilt is a large item clear a space on the floor to work on or spread the quilt over a large table.

1 Lay the backing sheet down first, RS underneath.
2 Lay the wadding sheet on top of this.
3 Lay the quilt top RS up on top of the wadding so that the extra material is distributed evenly round the edge.
4 Using a large needle and buttonhole thread join the 3 layers of the quilt together on the points marked

on Fig 3. When stitching through leave enough thread trailing to tie into a triple knot on the back of the quilt. Cut the threads off not too close to the knot. This is the easiest way to join the layers but a quality touch would be to make lines of hand stitching (proper quilting) between the diamonds. Bear in mind that this is very time-consuming and the child might well have grown up by the time the quilt is completed!

5 Tack the 3 layers of the quilt together at the edges keeping the stitching lines straight whilst leaving 1cm (½in) SA on the top quilt.

Border (Fig 4)

1 Cut 4 strips of binding ribbon to fit the edges of the quilt. They should be the length of each edge plus the width of the ribbon at each end (satin binding ribbon suitable for trimming blankets is usually 8cm (3in) wide and comes ready folded).

2 Treat top and bottom edges of the quilt first. Sew one edge of the ribbon to the back of the quilt on the seam line with the extra ribbon jutting out at the ends. Open out the ribbon.

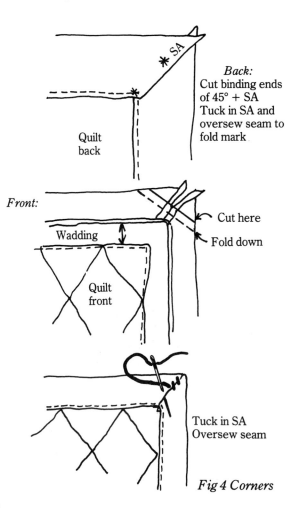

Back:
Cut binding ends of 45° + SA
Tuck in SA and oversew seam to fold mark

* SA

Quilt back

Front:

Cut here

Fold down

Wadding

Quilt front

Tuck in SA
Oversew seam

Fig 4 Corners

65

CF

Place to fold

Appliqué pieces

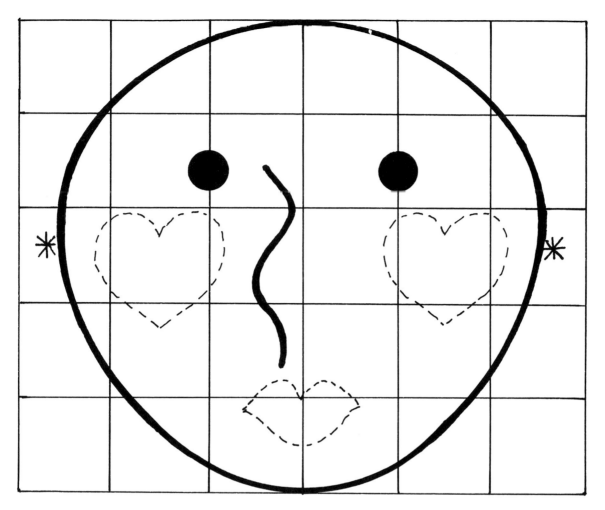

¹/₂ size: enlarge squares to 5cms (2in)

3 Sew the longer ribbons in the same way to the sides of the quilt.

4 Trim the wadding and sheet down evenly to 4cm (1½in) (or half the width of the ribbon).

5 Turn the ribbon onto the front of the quilt, mitre the corners and stitch down the free edge on the line. A zig-zag machine stitch is ideal for this.

Decoration

1 Enlarge face pattern from grid above and trace off other appliqué pieces opposite.

2 Transfer patterns to fabrics.

3 Place wadding square onto muslin square for backing.

4 Sew the appliqué pieces in this order: hat, then face piece, then features. Deline the nose. Use black thread and buttonhole stitch (see page 10).

5 Trim away spare backing.

Frill

1 Using string and chalk method (see page 7), draw a circle on the net 1m (40in) diam.

2 Make the puff frill (see page 15).

3 Spread the gathers evenly and place the clown's face onto the frill slightly higher than the centre. Tack round the edge of the motif.

4 Position the decoration on the quilt in the bottom righthand corner 64cm (25in) in from the side, 76cm (30in) up from the base.

5 With hand stitches through the black outlines catch the decoration to the quilt top at strategic places. The outer edge of the frill remains loose.

For extra sparkle a scattering of sequins can be glued onto the net of the frill.

─────────────

Overleaf (left to right): Ribbon Cushion; Covered Coat-Hanger; Harlequin Quilt; Pyjama Case (Pierrot version); Dressing-Table Doll

PYJAMA CASE

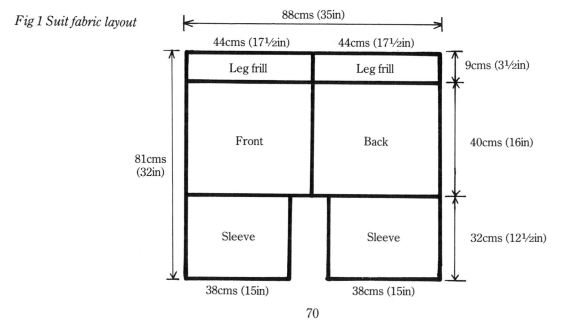

Children will love this bright and cheerful pyjama case clown. Soft and cuddly, he has no hard bits and is safe for a young boy or girl. If made in the materials suggested he is then machine washable (on a low programme), so he makes an ideal container for night clothes during the day or plumped up with a tee shirt at night. Any bright, plain or patterned cotton will do but as red is a notoriously difficult colour to match try to avoid different reds close together. The red nose is essential.

Throughout this pattern the stockinette is cut double and treated as one layer. The neck frill measures 84cm (33in) but wait until the suit is made up before cutting out to allow for any variation in the top of the suit; your seams may not be so perfect and even an inch out may mean cutting another frill. Tread carefully.

For the adventurous needleworker, an alternative design is illustrated in the photograph on pp68-9. With his creamy satin suit and heart-shaped cheeks, this happy Pierrot is the perfect addition to any lovestruck teenager's bedroom.

MATERIALS

30cm (12in) square of flesh-coloured stockinette
12cm (5in) square of iron-on interfacing
2 black felt circles 2cm (¾in) diam
2 white felt circles 2cm (¾in) diam
1 bright red pompon 4cm (1½in) diam
25g (1oz) bright yellow DK wool
50cm (20in) white cotton fabric 114cm (45in) wide
1m (1yd) bright red bias binding 1cm (½in) wide
46cm (18in) square bright red cotton fabric
1m (1yd) striped cotton fabric (ticking) 92cm (36in) wide
27cm×56cm (11×22in) plain blue cotton fabric
23cm (9in) ready-made popper-tape (snap fastener tape) 2cm (¾in) wide
Red, white and blue sewing threads
Black embroidery thread; black sewing thread and white button thread
25g (1oz) white 3-ply wool
Copydex adhesive
200g (8oz) toy filling
75cm (30in) soft white elastic ½cm (¼in) wide
2m (2yd) white bias binding 1cm (½in) wide

Fig 1 Suit fabric layout

88cms (35in)

44cms (17½in)   44cms (17½in)

| Leg frill | Leg frill | 9cms (3½in) |

| Front | Back | 40cms (16in) |

81cms (32in)

| Sleeve | Sleeve | 32cms (12½in) |

38cms (15in)   38cms (15in)

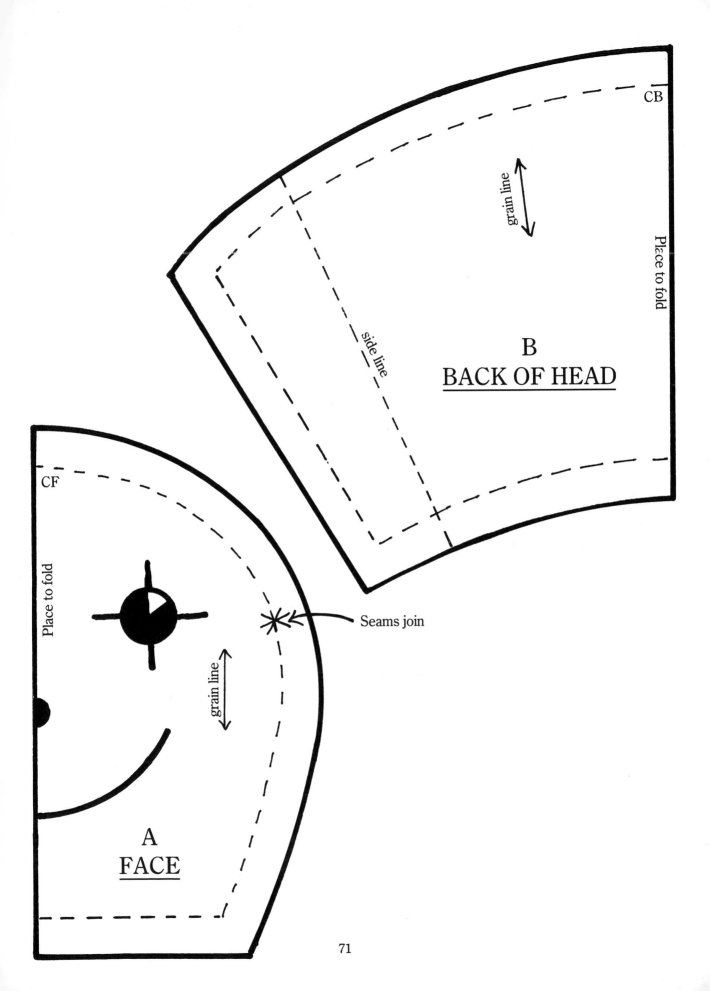

CB

grain line

Place to fold

side line

B
BACK OF HEAD

CF

Place to fold

grain line

Seams join

A
FACE

METHOD

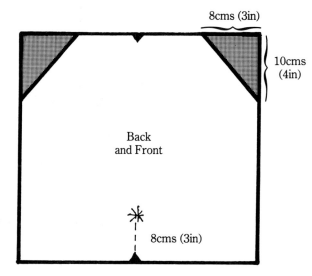

1 Make pattern (see page 71, 74-5) and transfer pattern pieces to fabrics.
2 Cut piece A once in stockinette.
3 Cut piece B once in stockinette.
4 Cut piece C once in blue fabric.
5 Cut piece D once in blue fabric.
6 Cut piece E twice to the fold of white fabric leaving enough for a strip 13cm (5in) deep.
7 Cut piece F 4 times out of red fabric (2 pairs).
8 Cut piece G twice out of red fabric.
9 Using the layout in Fig 1, cut the suit fabric. Open the fabric out and use one way for vertical stripe. Cut away shaded areas as shown in Fig 2 (There is 1cm (½in) SA on the pattern pieces.)
10 Mark the features on the face, the openings and placket lines on the suit, and the opening on the body.
11 Iron on the interfacing of the face avoiding the seam lines.

8cms (3in)

10cms (4in)

Back and Front

8cms (3in)

10cms (4in)

9cms (3½in)

Sleeve

6cms (2½in)

Fig 2 Cut aways

12 Embroider the face by hand or machine using black stem stitch for the mouth. Make the eyes (see page 13) and sew crosses over them with black thread.
13 Securely stitch the pompon to the face. Stay-stitch round the face.

Hair

1 Cut strands of wool for hair 12cm (5in) long (see page 14).
2 Stay-stitch round piece B and apply hair to top curve on seam line avoiding SA at sides. Start the stitching in the centre of the seam to keep both sides even. Fold back the wool to show SA.

Head

1 Join back of head to back of hat RS tog. Sew round enclosing the hair in the seam.
2 Join front of hat to face RS tog.
3 Join front of head to back of head RS tog keeping the hair out of the way and matching up fabrics at sides of head.
4 Top-stitch the horizontal line on the hat.

Body and arms

1 Place 2 body pieces RS tog.
2 Sew round leaving open at neck and base. Clip curves.
3 Place the body over the head RS tog and sew round neck seam.
4 Turn out the body, arms and hands. Poke out the thumbs with a pencil.
5 Stuff the body, arms and hands with toy filling starting with the hands, then the head and lastly the body.
6 Oversew the opening, tucking in the SA at the same time.

At this stage it is convenient to trim the hair down to 8cm (3in) and give the clown a good shake.

Boots

1 Make the boots as three-piece boots (see page 16).
2 Close the top openings from side to side so the toes point forwards.

Leg Frills

1 Make French seams (see page 16) at the short end of each frill.
2 Turn up a narrow hem on bottom edge.
3 Gather up the other edge to fit the tops of the boots comfortably.
4 Have the seams towards the inner sides of the boots. Tack across on the seam line so boots are enclosed by the frills.

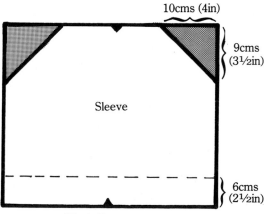

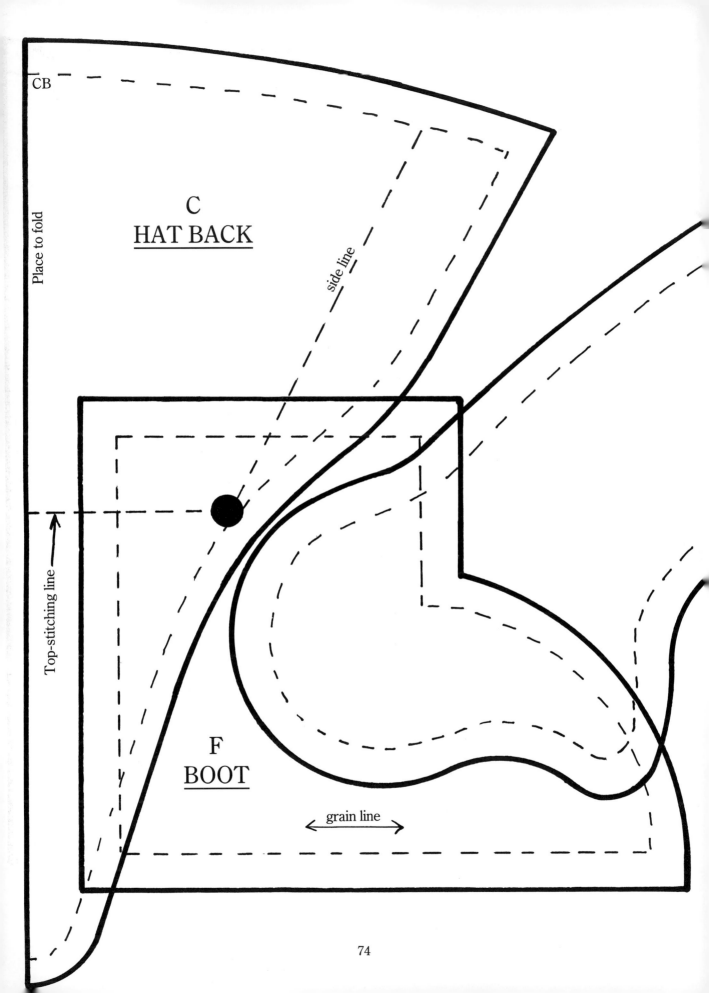

CB

Place to fold

C
HAT BACK

side line

Top-stitching line

F
BOOT

grain line

74

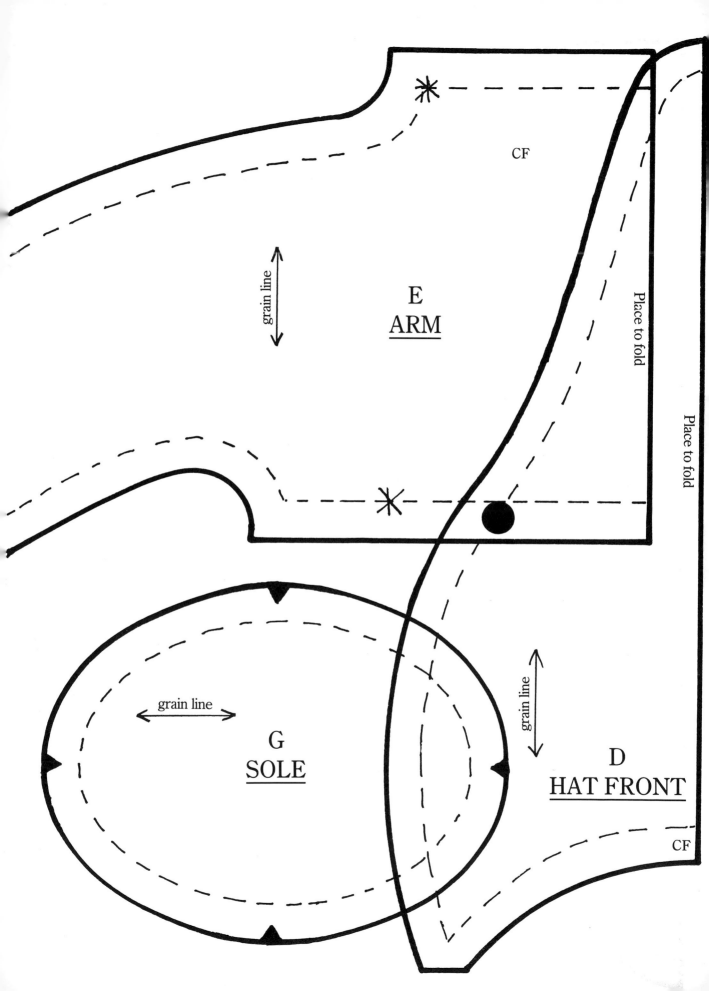

Suit

1 Place 2 pieces of suit RS tog.
2 Sew whole of left-hand seam and first 8cm (3in) and last 8cm (3in) of right-hand seam, leaving space for popper placket.
3 Sew the crotch seam and clip the SA.
4 Clip the SA at the top and bottom of placket opening.
5 Sew popper tape in position (see Fig 3). Front tape goes WS of tape to RS of front suit; sew on seam line, turn to inside and sew down. Back tape goes WS of tape to RS of suit; sew on seam line. Leave protruding so poppers can be fastened. Sew tapes down onto the front suit at top and bottom of opening.

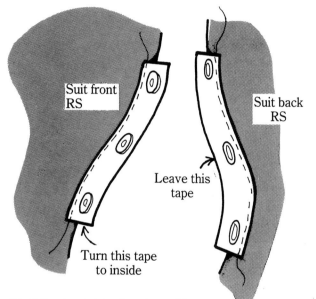

Suit front RS

Suit back RS

Leave this tape

Turn this tape to inside

Fig 3 Sewing popper tape in position

Sleeves

1 Turn up a narrow hem at the bottom of each sleeve.
2 Fold the sleeves in half RS tog and sew underarm seam.
3 Join sleeves to suit RS tog matching seams.
4 Make casing for elastic with white bias tape on placket line of each sleeve (see page 9).

Legs

1 Gather the leg openings of the suit to fit the tops of the boots.
2 Place the legs over the boot tops, RS tog.
3 Sew firmly across the layers on the seam line taking in all thicknesses of suit openings, leg frills and boot tops.
4 Turn out the suit.

Neck frill

1 Make sure the frill will fit the suit.
2 Apply red bias binding to one edge of the strip.
3 Make a French seam (see page 16) at one end. (This goes at the back.)
4 Place WS of frill to RS of suit and sew round.
5 Make placket for neck elastic with white bias tape.
6 Thread elastic to fit neck through the neck placket and elastic to fit wrists through wrist plackets. Secure the ends of the elastic with weaver's knots. (see page 9).
7 Push the clown into the suit through the side opening and put his arms into the sleeves. Pull the gathers into place at wrists and neck.
8 Make the tassel for his hat (see page 14) and sew firmly to the point of the nightcap.

MACHINE

RIBBON CUSHION

This bright, cheerful design would suit a little boy's room. The background fabric is created by sewing ribbons in a diagonal across a square of strong cotton material. The ribbons used are the very cheap sort of satin ribbon without a woven edge. They are usually readily obtainable in a variety of bold colours. The same method of applying the ribbons can be used to create other items, eg a quilt cover, borders at the bottom of curtains etc. For a quilt cover make a series of squares decorated with the diagonal stripe and join them together, with the lines going different ways perhaps, then make the lining and backing as for the Harlequin Quilt on page 63.

The clown face motif can also be made into a stencil if desired, enlarged or made smaller, and applied to cupboards and walls. You will need 1 stencil for each colour area.

MATERIALS

A piece of heavy bright red satin 43cm (17in) square

A piece of strong cotton fabric 43cm (17in) square

3m (3yd) heavy satin ribbon 8cm (3in) wide in red to match the satin or in a contrast colour

Assorted cheap satin ribbons 4cm (1½in) wide (buy 1m (1yd) of each of 6 or 8 different colours)

23cm (9in) square white felt

23cm (9in) square black felt

8cm (3in) square red felt

10cm (4in) square bright pink felt

30cm (12in) square lemon yellow felt

10cm (4in) square purple felt

Iron-on interfacing 43cm (17in) square

Red sewing thread, black sewing thread, beige sewing thread

250g (8oz) cushion filler, toy filler or Kapok

METHOD

1 Make templates for appliqué pieces by tracing off page and transferring to felt colours. Cut face shape from white felt; 2 circles 1cm (½in) diam from black felt; 1 circle 5cm (2in) diam from red felt; 2 circles 4cm (1½in) diam from bright pink felt; frill shape from lemon yellow felt; and 1 circle 10cm (4in) diam from purple felt. Cut this into 2 equal halves for the hair shapes.

2 Back each shape with interfacing.

3 To make the design on the front of the cushion, start at one top corner of the cotton square with one short piece of ribbon in a chosen colour. Sew it in position. This first piece of ribbon goes WS down and must jut out over the point of the corner (Fig 1).

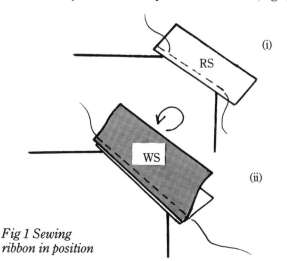

Fig 1 Sewing ribbon in position

4 Place the next piece of ribbon, in another colour, RS down on top of the first piece and make a line of stitches close to the edge of the ribbons. Fold the second ribbon back RS up and press.

5 Carry on in this way with the different colours of ribbon, each one being sewn down onto the previous one, folded back and pressed. It is important to cut the lengths of ribbon with enough to spare to cover the edge of the backing material – about the width of the ribbon at each end.

6 When the square is completely covered with ribbon sew down the decoration in this order:

  i) Frill (leave the top edge free of outline which would show through white felt)

  ii) Hair

  iii) Face

  iv) Features

Use black thread and buttonhole stitch. (For appliqué, see page 9-10.)

To make the frill

1 Join the ends of the red ribbon with a French seam (see page 16). Make sure the ribbon is not twisted.

2 Gather one edge of the ribbon to fit round the edge of the cushion.

3 Pin the frill on the seam line 1cm (½in) from the edge, RS tog (see Fig 2), with the fullness arranged evenly at each side. Allow a little extra at the corners.

4 Sew round on the seam line.

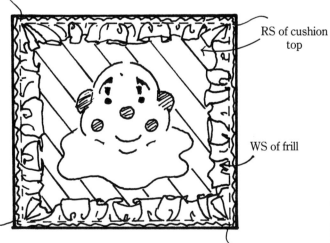

RS of cushion top

WS of frill

Fig 2 Attaching the frill

5 Place the red satin cushion back and the cushion front RS tog and sew round leaving an opening of about 20cm (8in) in the middle of one side.

6 Clip the corners, turn out through the opening and press the SA to the inside of the opening.

7 Stuff the cushion and close up the opening with oversewing by hand.

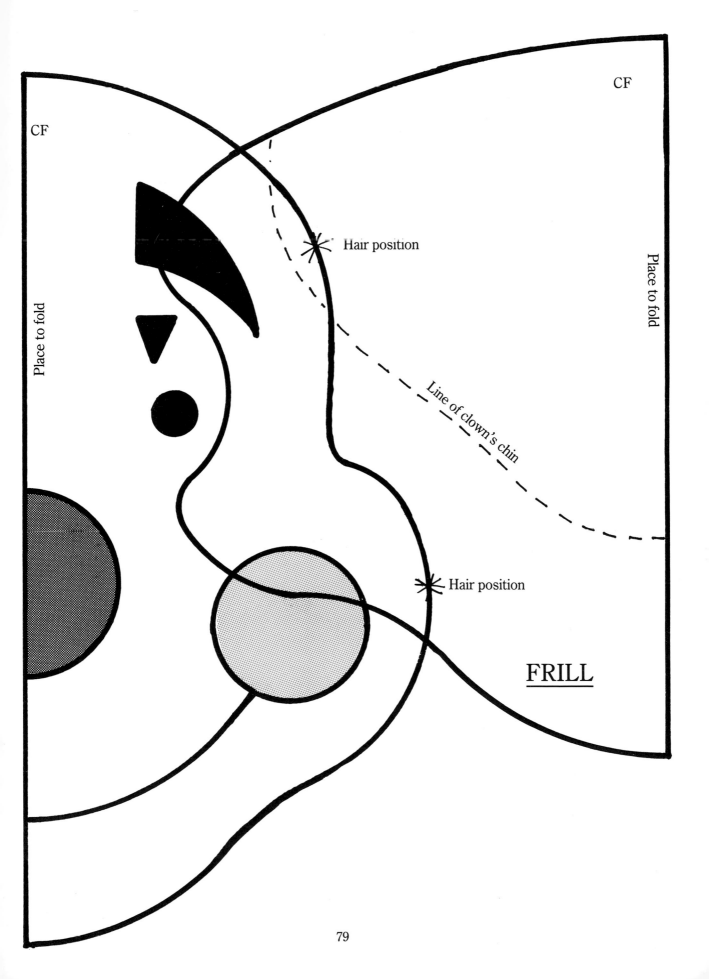

CF

CF

Place to fold

Place to fold

Hair position

Line of clown's chin

Hair position

FRILL

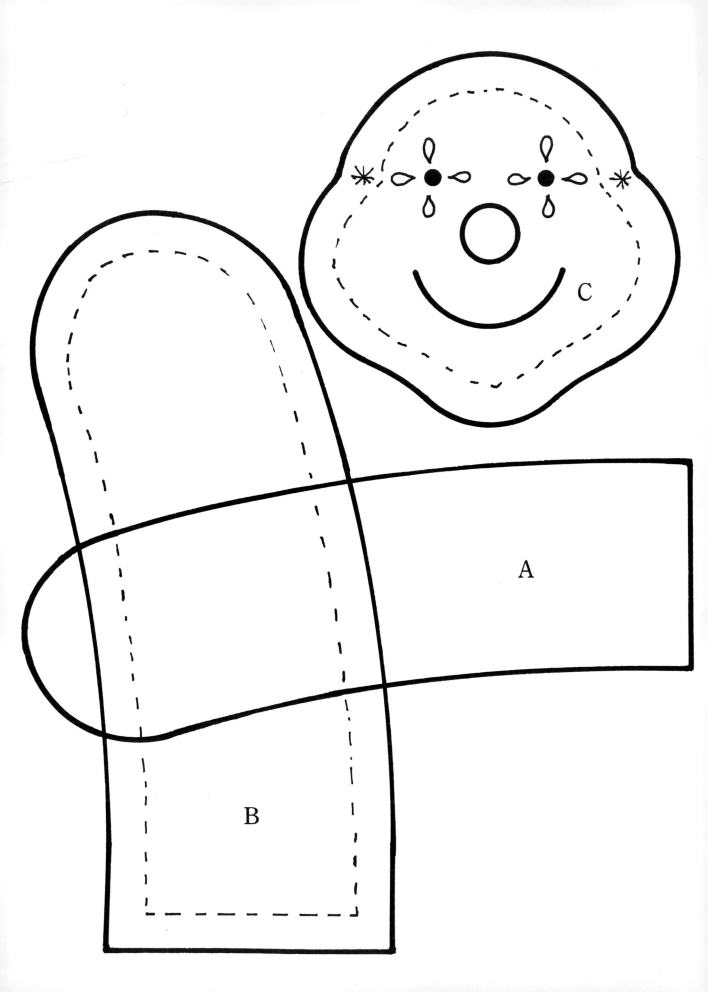

COVERED COAT-HANGER

These are ordinary wooden coat-hangers which, with clown decoration and padding, become a charming gift for a young child. The amounts of fabrics given are for covering one child-sized hanger; to cover a larger sized coat-hanger, just add half the measured difference to the CF and CB lines of the patterns. The clown head can be filled with lavender seeds, or a non-lumpy potpourri, or a ball of cotton wool sprinkled with perfume.

MATERIALS

36cm (14in) red dotted nylon 92cm (36in) wide
Plain white muslin 60cm×20cm (24in×8in)
Polyester wadding 30cm×40cm (12in×16in)
A small piece of iron-on interfacing 10cm (4in) square
A 30cm (12in) wooden coat-hanger with screw hook
15cm (6in) white satin ribbon 25mm (1in) wide
3.50m (3½yd) blue/green DK cotton
12cm (5in) square of white double stockinette
One handful of toy filler, cotton wool or 12g (½oz) potpourri or lavender seeds
Embroidery threads in black, red, white and yellow
25cm (10in) of bright yellow ribbon 1cm (½in) wide

METHOD

1 Make patterns (opposite).
2 Transfer patterns to fabrics.
3 Cut out A in wadding 8 times.
4 Cut out B in dotted nylon 4 times.
5 Cut out B in muslin 4 times.
6 Cut 2 strips of dotted nylon 8cm (3in) wide, 92cm (36in) long. (A SA of 1cm (½in) is included.)

To cover the hook (see Fig 1).
1 Unscrew the hook from the hanger.
2 Fold the satin ribbon in half along its length, RS tog.
3 Close off one end by sewing across in a slight curve.
4 Turn out and press, WS tog.

Fig 1

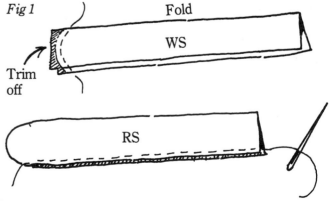

81

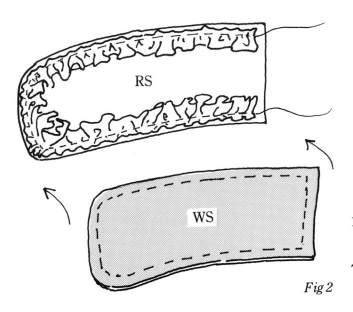

RS

WS

Fig 2

5 Run a gathering thread along the open edge of the ribbon.
6 Place the ribbon sock over the hook with the gathers to the inner curve and pull up the gathers to fit the hook closely.
7 Finish off the thread securely.

To pad out the hanger
1 Place the wadding shapes on the arms of the hanger, 2 front and 2 back on each arm.
2 Stab-stitch round close to the edge of the wood.
3 Trim the wadding down to within ½cm (¼in) of the stitching.
4 Butt the wadding together at CF and CB (see page 7, Sewing information).

To cover the hanger
The top covering for the hanger is made in the form of two frilled 'socks' which can be pulled onto the padded hanger at each side.
1 Keep the pieces in correct pairs.
2 Back each nylon piece with a muslin shape and sew round within the SA.
3 Fold the frill strips in half lengthways and gather along the edge. Pull up the gathers to fit each half sock.
4 Arrange the gathers evenly and pin on the seam line of each half sock RS tog with the folded edge of the frill pointing inwards (see Fig 2).
5 Pin the corresponding half sock RS down onto the frilled sections. Tack round. Leave the ends open beyond the SA at the centres.
6 Stitch round both socks.
7 Trim the SA to ½cm (¼in) and turn the socks out.
8 Pull the socks over the wadded arms of the hanger to meet in the middle.
9 Tuck in the SA at CF and CB and oversew.
10 Screw in the covered hook and join the hook cover to the hanger covering with a few small stitches.

To make the clown face
1 Trace off pattern shape C. Transfer to double stockinette and cut out once. (A 1cm (½in) SA is included.)
2 Back 1 face piece with interfacing and embroider the features (see pages 10-11).
3 Work in daisy stitch in black for the eyes, satin stitch in red for the nose, stem stitch in black for the mouth.
4 Cut the cotton strands for the hair, 10 for each side, each 15cm (6in) long.
5 Sew the hair in place on the seam line where marked. Trim the hair to 5cm (2in) at each side or leave long and make 2 plaits.
6 Cut a small slit in the back head piece before sewing up the head.
7 Tuck the hair out of the way and place front and back head RS tog.
8 Sew all the way round enclosing hair in seam. Trim SA.
9 Turn the head out through the back slit.
10 Press softly and stuff with chosen filling.
11 Oversew the back slit to close.
12 Attach head to hanger at CF to cover the join. Sew at places marked.
13 Make a bow out of yellow ribbon and attach it to the cover under the clown's chin.

PIERROT POWDER BOX AND PUFF

This pretty and useful present can be made from odds and ends left over from other projects. All you will need to buy is a pack of favourite body talc to put in the box. The face of the clown is made from small pieces of black and white felt and the frill can be made of net or chiffon, whichever is available. The puff is based on a set of circles using a clever method of sewing and turning.

When gift wrapping, different decorative stickers can be used, eg hearts, flowers or simple dots.

MATERIALS

For the box

1 empty cylindrical container 8.5cm (3¼in) diam (a popular custard-powder pack is ideal). The sides must be cardboard and the base cardboard or metal

A piece of black Fablon (stickyback plastic) 6cm×28cm (2½×11in) for covering the outside of the box

A piece of white Fablon 5×28cm (2×11in) for lining the box (amounts will vary depending on the type of container so check your dimensions first)

Approx 24 silver star stickers

Gloss paint: black and white

A thick, soft paintbrush

Marker pen, craft knife and fine sandpaper

Teazle or wire brush

For the puff

A piece of pink net 20cm (8in) square

A piece of pink fur fabric 15cm (6in) square

A piece of pink satin 15×38cm (6×15in)

Iron-on interfacing 20cm (8in) square

A scrap of black felt 5cm (2in) square

A scrap of white felt 5cm (2in) square

12cm (5in) turquoise satin ribbon ½cm (¼in) wide

Embroidery threads in pink, dark pink, black and silver

Copydex adhesive

Cellophane for wrapping

METHOD

To make the box

1 Dust out the empty container and discard the lid.

2 Draw a line round the drum 5cm (2in) up from the base. Cut the box along this line and smooth the edge with sandpaper.

3 Paint the outside base of the box with black gloss and leave to dry overnight.

4 Paint the inside base with white gloss. It may need a second coat.

5 Cover the outside of the box with the black Fablon leaving 1cm (½in) jutting out beyond the top edge.

6 Clip this allowance every 1cm (½in) along and fold the flaps down onto the inside of the box.

7 Cover the inside of the box with white Fablon placing the top edge of the lining just under the extreme edge of the box.

8 Decorate the outside surface with stickers.

To make the puff

1 Cut pattern piece A twice in pink satin.

2 Cut 1 circle of pink satin, 1 of interfacing and 1 of fur fabric, each 11cm (4¼in) diam.

3 Cut 1 circle of pink net 19cm (7½in) diam. (The SA allowed is 1cm (½in).)

4 Place 2 half moon shapes (A) RS tog and sew along stitching line of lesser curve.

5 Trim down SA close to stitching. Turn out so WS tog and press. Treat as one layer.

6 Iron the interfacing onto the reverse of the satin circle. Draw round the stitching line for guidance when sewing.

7 Make a 5cm (2in) horizontal slit in the circle at one side for turning the puff through (this will be hidden when the puff is finished).

8 Place the layers of the puff in a sandwich as in Fig 1. Check that the slit in the circle is positioned over the half moon.

9 Sew round the sandwich on the seam line. Carefully trim the SA down close to the stitching.

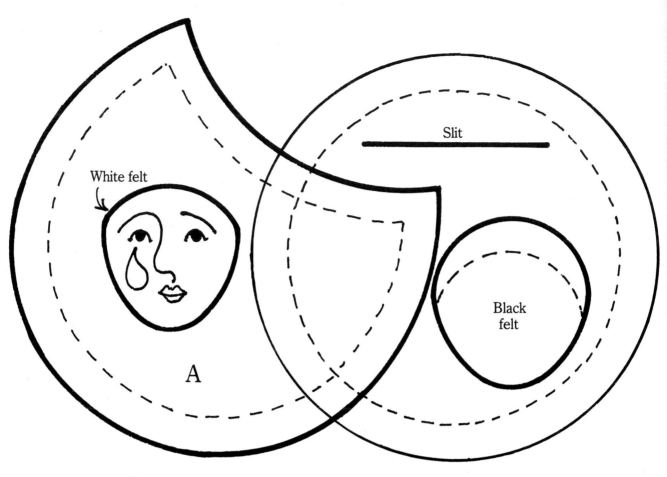

White felt

Slit

Black felt

A

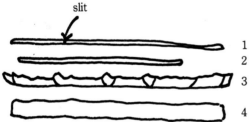

slit

1
2
3
4

Fig 1: Puff sandwich. Top layer: satin circle, RS down; 2nd layer: half moon; 3rd layer: fur fabric, fluff side up; bottom layer: wadding

10 Turn the puff through the slit, then turn the half moon section over onto the back to form a pocket and hide the slit.

11 Push out the edge with a blunt pencil and press the puff gently with a warm iron.

12 Brush the fur fabric with a teazle brush or wire brush to fluff it up (avoid catching the satin during the process).

Decoration

1 Transfer the face and hat sections to the felts.

2 Cut them out and iron them in position on the interfacing.

3 Sew round the edges with black embroidery thread.

4 Outline the features with three strands of thread in tiny back stitches. Fill in the mouth and tear spaces with satin stitch.

5 Trim away the excess interfacing.

6 Make a puff frill with the net circle (see page 15).

7 Place the pierrot's head onto the frill covering the centre point.

8 Sew round the outline of the head to fasten it to the frill.

9 Centre the frill on top of the puff and catch it to the half moon with a few small stitches through the outline of the head.

10 Make a little bow from the narrow ribbon and fasten it to the frill with a dab of glue.

11 Fill the box with powder (in a cellophane bag).

12 Place the puff on top and cover the box with cellophane. You will need a circle of about 24cm (11in) diam. Place the box face down in the centre of the circle and pleat the wrapping round the sides and onto the base. Fasten the pleats with a round sticker or piece of Sellotape.

13 Place a few stickers on the wrapping to frame the clown's face.

Bathroom Clowns (clockwise from left): Pierrot Powder Box and Puff; Scented Hanging Clown; Toilet Bag and Soap Sachet

SCENTED HANGING CLOWN

This clown is suitable for hanging in the bathroom or toilet or even inside the car. Different herb mixtures can be used as a filling to lightly perfume the air. A stronger accent can be made by filling the doll with ground cloves. Take care when using glitter fabric as it is very friable and should be backed with muslin. Alternatively, make up the suit from thin cotton with a tiny flower print.

MATERIALS

1×15cm (6in) square of black felt
1×15cm (6in) square of white felt
A piece of glitter (metallic thread) fabric 46×25cm (18×10in)
A piece of white muslin 46×25cm (18×10in)
30cm (12in) of white satin ribbon, 3mm (⅛in) wide
25cm (10in) of pink satin ribbon, 1cm (½in) wide
30cm (12in) of pink lace edging, 25mm (1in) wide
Embroidery thread in black, white, pink and dark pink
20cm (8in) square of pale pink nylon net
20cm (8in) square of white organdie or chiffon
About 2 handfuls of toy filling
3×1cm (½in) diam small black pompons or bobble-buttons
Use of 3 small elastic bands
About 50g (2oz) lavender seeds, cloves, potpourri etc, for filling
Watercolour paint (carmine)
Wide funnel

METHOD

1 Cut 1 circle each of pink net and white chiffon, 20cm (8in) diam.
2 Cut out piece A twice in white felt.
3 Cut out piece B 4 times in white felt.
4 Cut out piece C twice in black felt.
5 Cut out piece D 4 times in black felt.
6 Make pattern for suit (opposite). Cut out piece

E twice in suit fabrics (½cm (¼in) seam allowance is included).
7 Transfer features to face.
8 Embroider face thus: 3 bullion stitches in dark pink for mouth, 2 for top lip, 1 for bottom lip. Nose in black thread using small back stitch. Eye is a French knot at centre with straight stitches radiating outwards in black.

Head

1 Place head pieces RS tog and sew round leaving open at neck edge. Include the very narrowest ribbon in a loop at the top centre.
2 Turn out the head and stuff lightly with a little toy filling.
3 Close up neck opening on seam line.
4 Sink eyes (see page 13).
5 Sew 2 sides of hat together leaving a small space at top centre. Push the ribbon loop through this hole and settle the hat on the doll's head. Put a stitch through the top of the hat and the loop to secure.
6 Colour the cheeks with a spot of carmine watercolour and dab with water to disperse colour softly.
7 Make puff frills from net and chiffon (see page 15). Place them over the doll's head with the neck SA showing. Place an elastic band over the frills to keep them out of the way.

Hands and boots

1 Sew hands together in pairs leaving wrists open. Sew close to the edge of the felt.
2 Pad out the hand with wisps of toy filling.
3 Cut the pink lace edging into two equal parts and make a frill for each wrist by gathering one edge of each piece and pulling up to fit wrists.
4 Place a frill over each hand and put elastic bands over them.
5 Make boots in the same way without frills.

Suit

1 Back each glitter fabric section with muslin and treat as one fabric.
2 On RS of front sew hands and feet in position (see Fig 1).

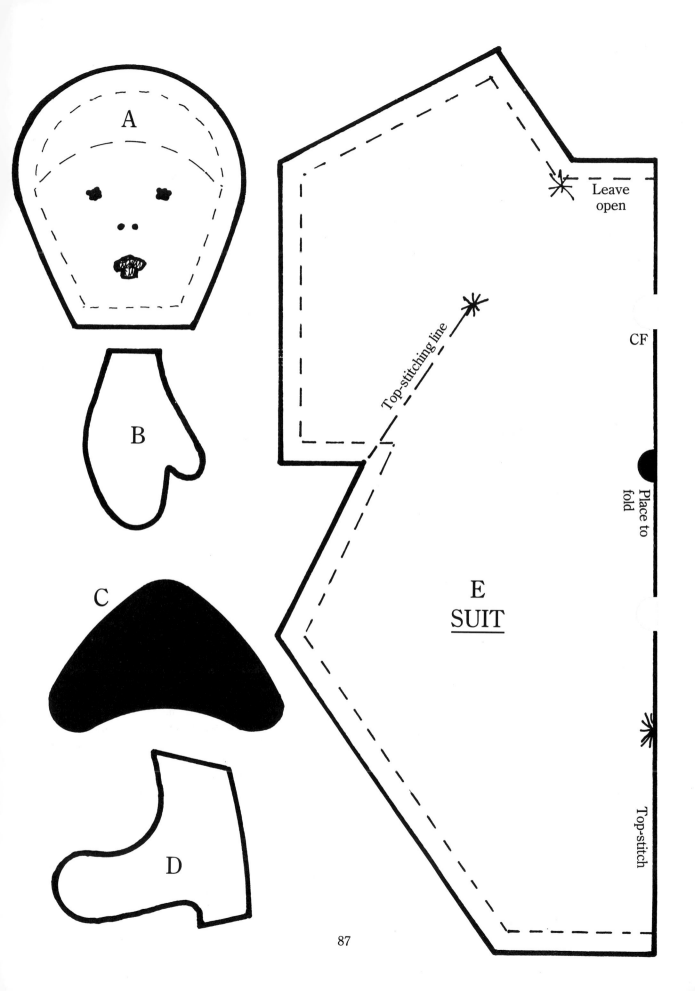

A

B

C

D

E
SUIT

Leave open

CF

Place to fold

Top-stitching line

Top-stitch

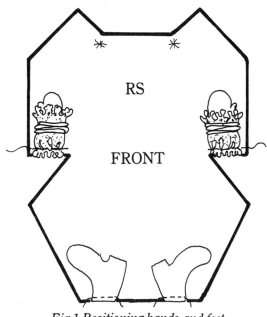

Fig 1 Positioning hands and feet

3 Place suit front and back RS tog and sew round all edges except neck opening. Take care not to trap the lace in the stitching.

4 Trim SA and clip corners.

5 Turn out the suit through the neck opening and carefully poke out the corners.

6 Top-stitch the lines at arm and leg divisions.

7 Using a wide funnel, tip the chosen filling into the bag of the suit.

8 Stuff the arms and shoulders with toy filling. The neck area should remain fairly flat.

9 Tuck in the SA at neck and push the head, with frills, into the neck opening.

10 Top-stitch across through all layers.

11 Glue on 3 pompons at CF.

12 Make a neat bow from the pink ribbon.

13 Press the neck frills down at the front and up at the back. Sew the bow in place under the doll's chin, going through to the back of the neck.

14 Trim the ribbon ends to points.

TOILET BAG AND SOAP SACHET

This bathroom set is bright, practical and fun to take on holiday or a cheerful holder for little necessities during a stay in hospital. The fabric used – colourful cotton with the addition of bright cord and jaunty pompons – has the spirit of the clown.

The bag and sachet are lined with thin, soft white plastic (vinyl) to keep them waterproof. The bag is wadded and can be quilted if desired.

MATERIALS (for bag and sachet)

40cm (15½in) bright yellow cotton with white polka dot (92cm (36in) wide
23cm (9in) polyester wadding 92cm (36in) wide
23cm (9in) white muslin 92cm (36in) wide
38cm (15in) white plastic lining 92cm (36in) wide
1m (1yd) bright red bias binding 1cm (½in) wide
2m (2yd) fancy green and white silk cord
2 bright red and 2 white pompons 4cm (1½in) diam
Machine threads to match fabrics.

METHOD

Measure the fabrics required (see layout Fig 1). Note there are different amounts for different fabrics as the cuff of the bag is not padded. (NB There is a 25mm (1in) SA on the pieces except those for the lining of the bag. These have a SA of 1cm (½in).)

Bag

1 Sandwich the layers of the bag together and tack round within the SA. Tack across the placket line.
2 Place front and back of bag RS tog and sew up the side seams leaving gaps at each side for the placket. (The top line of the gaps is 4cm (1½in) down from the top edge of the bag. The opening in the seam is 2cm (¾in).)
3 Open the SA at each side of the seam and press.
4 Sew round the placket openings to keep them open.
5 Join the circle base to the sides, RS tog. Trim off

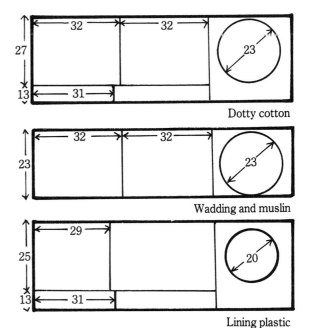

Fig 1 Cutting layout (figures in centimetres)

the excess SA to 1cm (½in) and turn out the bag.
6 The lining is made in the same way but without the openings in the side seams.
7 Slip the lining into the bag matching side seams.
8 Sew round on each placket line and the top edge.
9 Bind the top edge with red bias binding.
10 Thread the cord through the placket (see page 9).
11 Make or buy pompons and tie them onto the cords.

Soap sachet

1 Cut the strips of material and match them up, WS tog.
2 Bind the short ends with red bias.
3 Mark the position of the folds in the SA, 5cm (2in) and 20cm (8in) from top.
4 Fold the material (see Fig 2) in a pillow-slip closure.
5 Sew up each side on the seam line.
6 Turn out the sachet and poke out the corners.

Fig 2

MACHINE

JUG COSY

This jug (pitcher) cover will keep a container of milk or coffee warm whilst you wait. He could also cover a jug of punch on the Christmas table or fruit juice outdoors in summer. This size of cover will fit a jug about 23cm (9in) tall; a short version of the pattern can be made to cover a teapot. (A word of warning: do not *use him to cover hot pots when young children are about, as there is a great temptation for them to forget what is underneath him and treat the cosy as a toy, which is not intended.) Polyester boning in the hem keeps the suit open for ease of use and the white satin frill can be removed. The cosy is machine washable.*

MATERIALS

66cm (26in) green and white polka-dot cotton 92cm (36in) wide
33cm (13in) Polyester wadding 92cm (36in) wide
33cm (13in) muslin 92cm (36in) wide
A piece of flesh-coloured double stockinette 13cm (5in) long×28cm (11in) wide
20cm (8in) square of white polycotton
3 bright red pompons 4cms (1½in) diam
2 handfuls toy filling
25cm (10in) red bias binding 1cm (½in) wide
60cm (24in) red bias binding 25mm (1in) wide
60cm (24in) polyester boning (Rigilene)
25cm (10in) white lace edging 25mm (1in) wide
25g (1oz) orange DK cotton
25cm (10in) red satin ribbon ½cm (¼in) wide
50cm (20in) white satin ribbon 6cm (2½in) wide
2 circles of black felt 1cm (½in) diam
One circle of red felt 2cm (¾in) diam
Embroidery threads in black and white
Sewing thread in flesh, red and green
Copydex adhesive
8cm (3in) square iron-on interfacing

METHOD

1 Make patterns (opposite). Extend baseline of B for 8cm (3in).
2 Transfer patterns to fabrics.
3 Cut A twice from double stockinette.
4 Cut B 4 times in polka-dot cotton, twice in muslin and twice in wadding. Add another pompon position at CF.
5 Cut C 4 times in white polycotton.

(NB There is a SA of 1cm (½in) on head and hands and a SA of 25mm (1in) on B. Omit stay stitching on this design.)

Head

1 Treat double stockinette as single fabric and mark features on face. Back with a patch of interfacing. Embroider mouth in black stem stitch (see page 11). Embroider cheek lines in black back stitch.
2 Appliqué red nose in position and either glue or stitch eyes on face.
3 Cut orange cotton into 15cm (6in) lengths and apply to head (see page 14).
4 Sew narrow ribbon in a loop at CF top.
5 Place head pieces RS tog and sew round including hair in seam and leaving neck edge open.
6 Turn out head and stuff. Push stuffing well in, away from neck edge, and make little tucks in each side of the neck to narrow it down.
7 Close off neck on seam line.
8 Trim the hair down to 5cm (2in) making it slightly shorter at the sides. Hold the ribbon loop out of the way whilst cutting.

Hands

1 Place hands RS together in pairs.
2 Sew round leaving open at wrists.
3 Reduce SA, clip corners and turn out.
4 Press the hands and stuff them lightly.
5 Close off at the wrists on seam lines.

Body

1 On top layer of front fabric attach the hands with the thumbs pointing inwards. Keep clear of the SA at the sides.

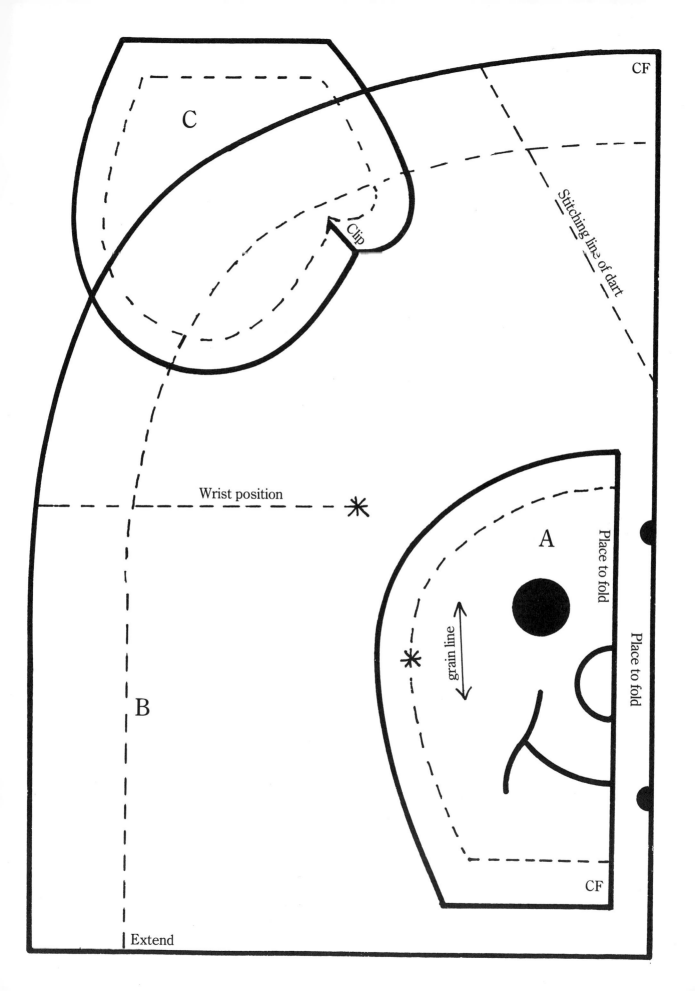

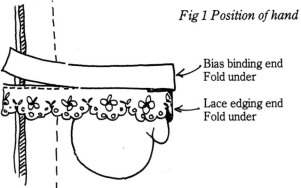

Fig 1 Position of hand

Bias binding end
Fold under

Lace edging end
Fold under

2 Cut the lace edging in two equal pieces and fold under a raw end on each piece.

3 Apply the pieces of lace over the hands (the lace carries on into the SA: see Fig 1).

4 Place front fabrics together in a sandwich: top fabric, then wadding, then muslin.

5 Tack together all round and also down centre of dart.

6 Cover the wrist edges with narrow bias binding, sewing through all layers.

7 Stitch pompons in place at CF through all layers.

8 Place back fabrics together in a sandwich and tack all round and down centre of dart.

9 Stitch darts in front and back body. Trim away and flatten the darts out.

10 Stitch head in place on RS of front.

11 Place back and front body RS tog matching darts at top.

12 Sew round curved seam and reduce SA to 1cm (½in).

Lining

1 Make darts in both lining pieces and place front and back linings RS tog matching darts at top.

2 Sew round curved seam and trim SA down to 1cm (½in).

Assembly

1 Place lining inside cosy, matching side seams.

2 Sew round base line through all layers and trim away excess SA.

3 Bend the boning into a circle to fit the base of the cosy, overlapping the ends, and secure the ends with glue, a metal staple or stitching.

4 Apply wide bias binding to base of cosy (see page 9). Include the circle of boning before the final stitching onto RS of cosy.

Neck Frill

Make a neck frill with white satin ribbon (see page 15) and pull up tightly round the clown's neck. Squeeze the head into shape.

COOK'S APRON

This unusual apron would make an excellent present for the cook in the family – male or female. It suits a large, jolly cook, the larger the better, being both amusing and practical. Bias tape outlines the design on a base fabric of tough blue denim whilst the lower half of the clown's face forms a pocket. A stuffed bow under his chin adds the finishing touch.

MATERIALS

A piece of heavy blue denim 92cm (36in) long×66cm (26in) wide

3m (3yd) bright green bias binding 1cm (½in) wide

64cm (25in) bright red petersham ribbon 4cm (1½in) wide (for neck strap)

150cm (60in) of same but only 1cm (½in) wide cut into 2 equal lengths for ties (NB If different widths of the same ribbon prove impossible to find use the narrower width for both parts)

50×70cm (20×28in) cream-coloured cotton drill or strong cotton

1m (40in) orange satin ribbon 1cm (½in) wide

2m (2yd) red bias binding 1cm (½in) wide

36×23cm (14×9in) green and white candy-striped cotton

1 handful of toy filling

A piece of black felt 30×12cm (12×5in)

A piece of white felt 12cm (5in) square

A piece of red felt 18cm (7in) square

Sewing threads in red and green to match bias tapes and black for appliqué lines

White crayon

METHOD

Apron

1 Fold the piece of denim in half lengthways.

2 Mark CF at top and bottom.

3 Measure along the top edge 13cm (5in) from fold.

4 Measure up the side edge 56cm (22in) from base.

5 Join these points with a sloping line.

6 Cut along this line and open out the apron.

7 Join the neck strap to the top corners and the tie ribbons at each side, leaving enough room to bind the edges of the denim.

8 Bind the whole edge of the apron with the green bias.

Appliqué

1 Make the patterns for the appliqué pieces (see pages 94-5).

2 Cut piece A (upper face) twice in cream drill.

3 Cut piece B (lower face) twice in cream drill.

4 Cut piece C (bow) twice, crossways, in green candy-stripe.

5 Cut pieces D and E (nose and mouth) once each in red felt.

6 Cut piece I twice in white felt.

7 From the black felt cut a strip for the moustache 30×8cm (12×3in) then cut pieces F, G and H twice each from the rest of the black felt.

(NB There is a SA of 1cm (½in) on the tie shape and the bottom edge of the upper face section. No SA is needed on the other pieces.)

8 Place two A sections RS tog. Sew along base line. Turn out and press, WS tog. Treat as one layer.

9 Bind the raw edge with red bias.

10 Mark the positions of eyes, nose and eyebrows on the face.

11 Sew the features to the face with black thread in buttonhole stitch.

12 Pin the face section to the apron at CF with the base on a line 50cm (20in) from the top edge.

13 Cut the orange ribbon into 8 equal lengths, fold each one in half and place them in bunches behind the face, 3 at each side and 2 at top centre.

14 Sew round the face on the bias tape enclosing the ribbon hair in the stitching.

15 Place the two B sections WS tog and bind the curved edge with red bias.

16 Fold the strip of black felt for the moustache over the edge of B to form a binding. Using white crayon, mark the outline of the moustache (J) and sew on

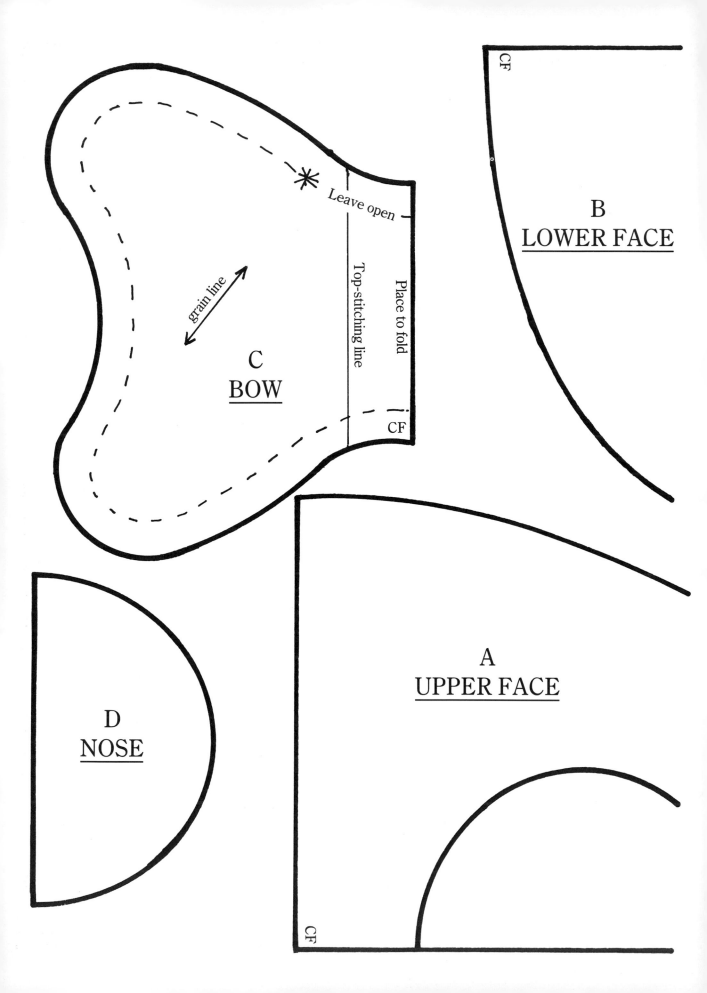

B
LOWER FACE

C
BOW

grain line

Leave open

Top-stitching line

Place to fold

CF

CF

D
NOSE

A
UPPER FACE

CF

CF

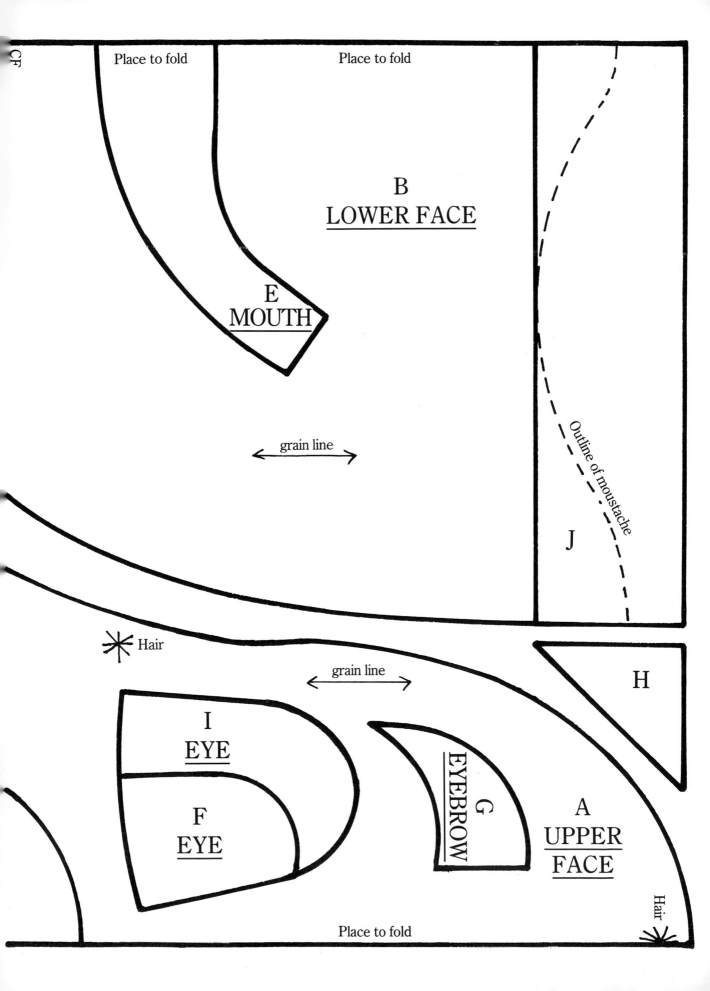

CF

Place to fold   Place to fold

B
LOWER FACE

E
MOUTH

grain line

Outline of moustache

J

✳ Hair

grain line

I
EYE

F
EYE

G
EYEBROW

A
UPPER
FACE

H

Hair

Place to fold

the outline through all thicknesses. Trim away the excess felt on both sides.

17 Using black thread apply the mouth section E in buttonhole stitch.

18 Pin the lower face to the apron to form a pocket, with the top edge just slightly overlapping the base of the upper face. Sew round the curve.

19 Sew a black felt triangle over each corner of the pocket at the join to strengthen and neaten.

Bow

1 Place 2 bow sections RS tog and sew round leaving opening as marked.

2 Clip the SA and turn out.

3 Stuff lightly with toy filling and close up the opening, tucking in the SA.

4 Press the bow lightly and place it on the apron in position under the chin.

5 Sew down on 'knot lines'.

HAND

SOUP CLOWN

This little clown is disguised as a 'bouquet garni'. The bag of his body holds a selection of herbs to be used for making stock. These herbs and spices can be mixed, or kept in single flavours such as rosemary, parsley, sage etc. You could even fill the body with tea leaves for a special 'cuppa', or mint leaves for a brew of mint tea. Make several clowns at once and keep them in a basket in the kitchen. One clown can be used two or three times: when a clown has lost his flavour, make a new body with fresh filling and attach it to an existing head.

MATERIALS

For one clown

1 plain wooden bead 2cm (¾in) diam (for head)

2 plain wooden beads 1cm (½in) diam (for hat pompon and neck stop)

Approx 35cm (14in) ribbon 3mm (⅛in) wide (for loop)

A piece of muslin or thin cotton 10cm (4in) wide×22cm (9in) long

Sewing thread to match

4 dried peas or butter beans

4×15cm (6in) lengths of bright-coloured knitting cotton or buttonhole thread

2 tbsp 10g of herb filling

A plastic icing nozzle

Small funnel

METHOD

Prepare the head first.

1 Thread the beads and the icing nozzle as in Fig 1.

2 Tie the ends of the ribbon in a double knot close to the hat bead to keep the components tight, then make a weaver's knot at the end (see page 9).

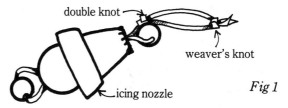

double knot

weaver's knot

icing nozzle

Fig 1

3 Fold the rectangle of fabric in half across RS tog and sew round, as far as the neck opening, at both sides. (The SA is ½cm (¼in).)

4 Turn out the bag through the neck opening and poke out the corners.

5 Push one pea or bean into each corner and tie off with the yarn. Wind the yarn round the 'limb' 3 times, then make a triple knot and trim the ends of the yarn down to about ½cm (¼in).

6 Run a gathering thread round the neck opening, tucking in the SA. Leave the thread trailing at both ends.

7 Fill the body with chosen herbs (use a funnel).

8 Insert the stop bead into the neck opening and pull up the gathering thread tightly round it. Tie off and trim the thread.

PEG PIERROT

These pretty little dolls can be adapted for many uses. Their bendy arms make them suitable for ring stands, or they could hold a bottle of perfume for a special present.

They are extremely economical to make; the basic doll is an old-fashioned wooden clothes peg, but they rely on neat painting and trimming which takes a bit of patience and time. It makes sense to paint a few dolls at once then if one is spoiled you can get on with the others.

MATERIALS

For one doll

1 clothes peg (dolly peg)
1 black chenille wire or pipe cleaner 5mm (¼in) wide
1 small block of black Fimo
20cm (8in) black satin bias ribbon 2cm (¾in) wide
25cm (10in) white satin ribbon 8cm (3in) wide
15cm (6in) double satin red ribbon 5mm (¼in) wide
15cm (6in) matching red ribbon 3mm (⅛in) wide
Embroidery threads in white, flesh and black
Delicate patterned white lace edging 2cm (¾in) wide and 1cm (½in) wide (15cm (6in) of each one)
Fine marker pens in red, white and black
White paint
Black paint
Clear varnish
Medium/fine sandpaper
Copydex adhesive
Plasticine
Craft knife
Small saw
2 sheets of writing paper
1 piece of card (postcard)

METHOD

1 Check that the peg is a good shape. Round off the head with sandpaper. Saw off the first 1cm (½in) of the 'legs' and smooth the ends. Have ready a blob of Plasticine to stand the doll on during painting. (For painting tips, see pages 12-13.)

2 Dip the head of the doll into white paint past the neck and let the paint run down the body of the peg. Stand the legs firmly in the Plasticine and leave to dry.

3 Dip the top of the head at an angle into the black paint, as far as the hat line. Allow the paint to run off at the back of the neck where it will not show. Leave to dry.

4 Remove any thick runs of paint with a craft knife.

5 Following Fig 1, mark in the features with black for the eyes and nostrils, red for the cheeks and mouth. Put the tiniest dot of white in the eyes for liveliness. Any mistakes can be painted over in white and repainted.

6 Apply 2 coats of clear varnish to head and neck.

Fig 1

Stand

1 Trace the stand pieces from Fig 2 and transfer to card. Cut out and use as a template. (One complete stand will take ⅛ of a standard block of Fimo so cut the block into 8 equal parts.)

2 Roll out a piece of Fimo and flatten it evenly to 5mm (¼in) (see page 12).

3 Cut round the templates.

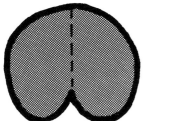

Base line

Fig 2 Stand pieces

4 Press the upright in position on the foot section and keep it at right angles with a thin worm of Fimo pressed into the angles at each side. Trim the stand and soften the edges gently with finger pressure. Bake as instructed.

5 Varnish the stand.

To assemble and dress the doll

For extra speed thread 2 needles with the flesh-coloured embroidery thread in lengths of 60cm (24in). Each one of these will cover a hand.

1 Cut the chenille wire to 11cms (4½in) long. Bend up the last ½cm (¼in) at each end for the hands.

2 Cover the bends with the flesh embroidery thread using close stitches going round and round into the centre hole until the black fluff is covered. To finish off, wind the thread round the wrist several times then pass the thread through the loops and pull tight. Cut the thread off close to the hand.

3 Cut the black satin bias into 3 equal pieces, 1 for each shoulder and 1 for round the body.

4 Fold the shoulder pieces in half lengthways. Holding the chenille arms against the back of the doll put the shoulder pieces in place, crossing at CF and CB. A dab of glue will hold them whilst you cover the ends with the third piece of bias wrapped round the body and overlapping at the back. Secure the back with a few stitches.

5 To make the baggy trousers, cut the white satin ribbon into 2 equal pieces.

6 For each leg, fold the ribbon in half RS tog with selvedges at top and bottom. Leaving a SA of 5mm (¼in), join this inside leg seam with running stitches leaving the top 3cm (1¼in) free. If necessary, oversew the edge to prevent fraying.

7 Turn out each leg to RS and pull them onto the doll's legs up to the waist.

8 At CB and CF tuck in the SA and join the two legs with a few small stitches, then join the trousers to the body covering at CF and CB.

9 With very small stitches gather up each side of the ribbon at the waist line close to the edge. Pull the gathers up tight and secure. Leave the trouser bottoms loose and puff the sides out.

10 Trim the waist with red satin ribbon made into a bow. Glue it to the CF of the trousers and cut the ends to points.

11 Make neck frill from the wider lace. Gather along one edge, very close, pop it over the doll's head and pull up tightly.

12 Cut the narrower lace into 2 equal halves and gather up each one as before. Fasten round the wrists with the lace falling over the hands. Cut the very narrow ribbon into 2 equal halves and tie one round each wrist, in a double knot, just above the lace cuff. Trim the ends to points.

13 Push the doll onto the stand. The upright has to go inside one of the trouser legs to be concealed.

14 Pose the doll's arms attractively by bending at wrists and elbows.

CHRISTMAS CLOWNS

These delightful little clowns look rather like snowmen when made up in white satin and silver glitter. They can be hung from the branches of a tree or pinned at intervals along a shelf or a mantelpiece. Alternatively, make them in different colours or shades of one colour. They are quite simple to make in quantity and unbreakable so they will last for many Christmasses.

MATERIALS

(to make 6 clowns)
Use best-quality white satin ribbon in different widths.

3mm (⅛in) wide: 150m (60in) for 6 hanging loops, each 25cm (10in) long

1cm (½in) wide: 192cm (2¼yd) for 24 small frills at wrists and ankles, each 8cm (3in) long

25mm (1in) wide: 120cm (1½yd) for 6 neck frills, each 20cm (8in) long

6cm (2½) wide: 120cm (1½yd) for 6 bodies, each 20cm (8in) long

6 small beads 1cm (½in) diam (for stops)

6 white beads 2cm (¾in) diam (for heads)

A string of glittery silver or gold beads (the type sold for decorations with the beads moulded onto the string allowing the rope to be cut into sections)

White paint (if the head beads need it)

Fine black marker pen

Clear varnish

1×15cm (6in) square white felt

1×15cm (6in) square iron-on interfacing

Copydex adhesive

Silver glitter pen or powder

Embroidery threads in white, bright yellow

2 handfuls of toy stuffing

24×1cm (½in) diam white bobble buttons for hands and feet

Christmas Clowns and a trio of Peg Pierrots

METHOD

1 Paint head beads white if necessary. Draw features on them. Varnish. (For painting beads, see page 13; for features, see Fig 1).

2 Thread loop ribbon down through head bead, through the stop bead and back through the head bead (see Fig 2). Tie a weaver's knot at the end (see page 9).

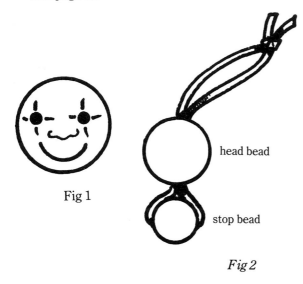

Fig 1

head bead

stop bead

Fig 2

3 Fold the piece of body ribbon in half WS tog and sew up each side close to the edge.

4 Stuff this pocket with a few pinches of toy stuffing.

5 Tuck in the top 1cm (½in) and oversew the edge whilst enclosing the stop bead on the head in the centre.

6 Make the neck frill, wrist and ankle frills (see page 15).

7 To make 1 foot, anchor a thread at the bottom corner of the suit. Pass thread through the ankle frill, through the hole in the bobble button, back through the frill to secure back at the corner of the suit. Repeat for other foot. Treat each hand similarly, attaching it to the edge of the suit about a third of the way down the side.

8 Attach the glitter beads to CF. Stitch below the top bead on the rope and above the bottom bead. Each clown should need about 9 beads depending on size.

To make hats and hair

1 Trace hat shape.

2 Back the felt with interfacing and cut out the hats.

3 Dot with glitter and allow to dry.

4 Cut lengths of yellow embroidery thread for hair. (Each clown will need about 28, each 3cm (1in) long.)

Hat shape

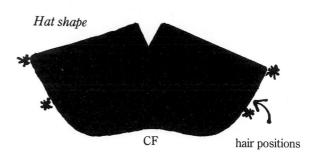

CF   hair positions

5 Note position of hair on bottom edge of hat. Spread a thin line of glue close to the edge on the WS. Stick the hair strands in position at each side and trim them evenly to 1cm (½in).

6 Curl the hat round the ribbon loop on the doll and oversew the CB seam close to the edge. The ribbon loop should run freely through the top notch.

7 Push the doll's head down onto his neck. Push his hat down onto his head and put a few stitches through the point of the hat into the loop to keep its position.

BROOCHES

These are all variations on the same basic pattern. A small decorated bas-relief face of Fimo is backed by a puff frill and mounted on a metal brooch-pin, the sort that has a flat disc on it. One block of Fimo is sufficient for 6 faces and some to spare. Cut the block into 4 equal parts and put one aside. Roll the other 3 parts into balls and cut them cleanly in half with a sharp knife. Each half ball has a 'stalk' of Fimo, which is cut out, using an apple corer, and pressed to the flat side of the face before baking.

The brooches look lovely pinned to the flap of an evening bag or on the lapel of a plain dress or jacket. Without the brooch-pin and with the addition of a loop of narrow ribbon at the back they can be used as room decorations. Hang one over the corner of a picture frame or mirror, or stick one to the lid of a sewing box or gift–wrapped box.

LITTLE WHITE-FACED CLOWN

MATERIALS

Half ball of Fimo (transparent type)
White paint
Black fine marker
2 small red stickers 5mm (¼in) diam
Clear varnish
A circle of white chiffon 15cm (6in) diam
White embroidery thread
Silver glitter pen or loose powder and glue
5cm (2in) gold ribbon ½cm (¼in) wide
15cm (6in) bright red double satin ribbon ½cm (¼in) wide
Copydex adhesive
Superglue
Plasticine
Paintbrush
Tweezers for handling stickers
Baking tray
Small piece of stiff card (postcard)
1 metal brooch-pin

METHOD

1 Make a 'stalk' out of the spare Fimo (ie a little round, flat cake 3mm (⅛in) thick ×1cm (½in) wide) to fit on the flat back of the face. There should be an even space all round the edge to allow the gathers of the frill to sit comfortably when the brooch is assembled.
2 Bake the Fimo as instructed.
3 Give the face 2 coats of white paint (see page 12).
4 Copy the features from Fig 1.
5 Varnish with clear varnish.

Fig 1

Frill

1 Decorate the white chiffon circle with silver glitter rings and dots.
2 Make it into a puff frill (see page 15).
3 Leave the gathers open enough to surround the stalk and cut a slit in the bottom layer so the stalk can appear.
4 Spread a small amount of superglue on the brooch pin and place the clown head carefully in position, making sure that the pin is horizontal.

Hat

1 Trace hat shape A from page 104.
2 Cut out the hat shape in card. Cover the surface with silver glitter.
3 Stick the hat on the clown's head at a jaunty angle resting close against the frill at the back.
4 Glue the gold ribbon to the edge of the hat.
5 Make a bow of the red satin ribbon and glue it under the clown's chin. Trim the ends to points.

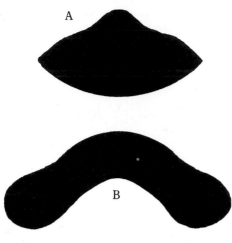

A

B

Hat shapes

A second type of frill can be applied to the same sort of face giving a totally different feeling to the design. Instead of white chiffon make a ribbon frill (see page 15) using 25cm (10in) of 25mm (1in) wide bright satin ribbon (eg tiny red dots on white or red and white check or stripe). Finish as the first brooch but omit the bow.

BLACK AND WHITE DOMINO

MATERIALS

Half ball of transparent Fimo
A little spare Fimo for modelling features
    and a stalk for behind the head
Painting materials as for Little White-faced
Clown (page 103) with the addition of some black paint
Cocktail sticks for modelling
A metal brooch-pin
A circle of black spotted net 18cm (7in) diam
Black embroidery thread
A small red rose (cake decoration)

METHOD

1 Mould a face in shallow relief (bas-relief)
2 Keeping the back of the Fimo flat, form it into an oval.
3 Press hollows for eye sockets with the end of a pencil and add small pieces of extra Fimo to the nose. Make nostrils with a cocktail stick.
4 To form the mouth and chin areas, press the side of the cocktail stick 3 times across the lower part of the face (see Fig 2).

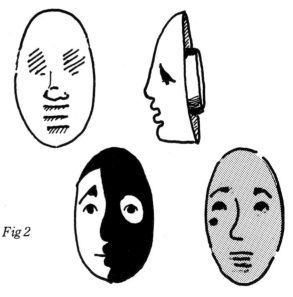

Fig 2

5 Press the cheeks in slightly and bake as instructed.
6 Cover the face with white paint and leave to dry. Divide it in half with a black line, then fill in half the face and the details with black paint (see Fig 2).
7 Make a puff frill and assemble as before.
8 Attach a small red rose to the frill underneath the clown's chin and slightly to one side.
    Alternatively, add a frill of stiff white satin ribbon instead of the net.

GOLD-FACED BROOCH

MATERIALS

Half ball of transparent Fimo
Some spare Fimo
Gold paint
Fine black marker pen
18cm (7in) diam circle of gold net
Gold-coloured embroidery thread
Very narrow satin ribbons in bright colours (eg pink,
    turquoise and lemon) cut into pieces approx 5cm
    (2in) long (2 of each colour)
Approx 5cm (2in) square black velour Fablon or felt
1 brooch back

METHOD

1 Model the face as for the Domino brooch
   and bake as instructed.
2 Paint the face gold all over. Allow to dry.
   Mark the eyes in black pen and add a
black beauty spot to the cheek.
3 Assemble the brooch as before.

Hat

1 Trace the hat shape B opposite.
2 Transfer the shape to the reverse of the Fablon or
   onto the felt. Cut out.
3 Curl the ribbon lengths by running tightly over the
   thumbnail at one side. Stick the tassel at the back of
   the hat at one side and stick the hat down onto the
   forehead at the front and the frill at the sides.

MASKS

Masks were very popular as fashionable accessories during the sixteenth and seventeenth centuries in England and on the continent, especially in Italy. Used partly to hide behind, in the same way as a fan, and partly as a screen against the sun, they were in their element in the theatre where their faces were symbolic of character – sad, happy, comic or grotesque. Nowadays we associate them mainly with pantomime and carnival time, for dressing up and disguise.

One of the most popular faces is that of the Venetian white-faced clown but a mask can be as simple or elaborate as you like. A lot of modern masks, eg those for stage shows, are made from fibreglass but the old-fashioned method using cloth, cane and glue is easier to follow at home. The method of construction for these masks is similar to the traditional one using a muslin shell on which paints, 'jewels' in the form of beads and sequins, can be laid. The plainer the mask the more difficult is the finishing; many bumps and blemishes can be hidden under the sequins but the white mask requires a smooth ground to paint on.

The cane handles can be omitted and the masks used as wall hangings, in which case put a ribbon loop at the top centre and don't bother to pierce the eye holes.

PREPARATION

The first step is to make a mould, a master shape, of a face. For this you will need:

A board for working on – an old tray or piece of plywood approx 30cm×40cm (12×16in)
2×500g (1lb) packs of modelling clay (Plasticine original waterproof formula doesn't shrink)
Marker pen
Ruler
Various modelling tools such as a sharp knife and a flat stick

1 To create an oval area on the board, make a vertical line halfway across the board. Make a horizontal line halfway up the board. Measure 12.50cm (5in) on each side of the centre point on the vertical. Measure 9cm (3½in) at each side of the centre point on the horizontal. Join these points with smooth curves to make an oval.

2 With the modelling clay fill this area with a shallow relief of the face. Start with large lumps pulled off the main mass for nose, cheeks, forehead and chin. Fill in the spaces with thumb-sized pieces then with smaller, fingernail-sized pieces. Be prepared to spend some time on this stage. There is a therapeutic effect in handling modelling clay so don't rush. Build up the face keeping it symmetrical and not too high or low in the peaks and hollows (this is termed 'bas-relief' in sculpture). Check the face from all angles. When satisfied with the shape finish off the surface by smoothing it with a flat stick. The surface of the clay will mould the inside of the mask so it does not have to be perfect, just no obvious bumps.

MATERIALS FOR BASIC WHITE MASK

1m (1yd) of white muslin 92cm (36in) wide
50g (2oz) cellulose paste mixed with 1L (2pt) of water
Vaseline petroleum jelly (to act as a releasing agent)
Approx 75cm (30in) piece of centre cane No 15 size
250ml (½pt) white oil-based paint
50g (2oz) plaster (dental plaster or Plaster of Paris)
Plastic filler paste
Medium sandpaper
Clear varnish
White buttonhole thread
Upholstery needle
Use of strong scissors, small craft saw, plastic bowl large enough to mix the paste in, bradawl (stiletto)

For the handle

A piece of garden cane 20cm (8in) long cut from the widest part of the cane

1 rawlplug (plastic wall plug) and round-topped screw to fit the hole in the cane

A plastic tap washer or circle of card 25mm (1in) diam

Additional items for painting masks

One 3cm (1in) paintbrush

A fine paintbrush (No 4)

Black paint and red paint, or gold paint plus an assortment of bright sequins and beads

Glue

Silver, gold or coloured glitter

Approx 75cm (30in) braid in silver or gold 2cm (¾in) wide

Satin ribbons for binding the cane handles

METHOD

1 Cut the muslin into 4 equal parts.
2 Mix the paste as directed.
3 Treat the surface of the mould with Vaseline.
4 Dip the pieces of muslin one by one into the paste. As you lift them out draw each one through a finger and thumb to remove excess paste.
5 Spread the muslins over the mould as smoothly as possible. Press out any air bubbles that form between the layers and carry the cloth over the edge of the mould and onto the board. Put each muslin on at a slightly different angle to the last one.
6 Leave the mask to dry for a few days. The muslin will tighten as the mask dries.
7 Remove the mask by cutting round the edge and pulling it away carefully. The master mould can be used again if required.
8 Make a loop out of the chair cane overlapping the ends for about 2cm (¾in) and binding the join with buttonhole thread.
9 Place the cane over the muslin shell with the overlap at the bottom centre. Draw round the inside of the loop to create the edge of the mask. Trim the excess fabric away on this line.
10 Fasten the chair cane to the edge of the mask by oversewing with buttonhole thread. Start at the top centre and work down each side to the chin keeping the shape even.

Handles

1 Cut one end of the piece of garden cane to a sharp angle corresponding to the angle of the mask at the chin.
2 Using a bradawl, or other sharp instrument, make a hole in the base of the mask.
3 Put the rawlplug in the top of the cane and the washer inside the mask over the hole. Line them up

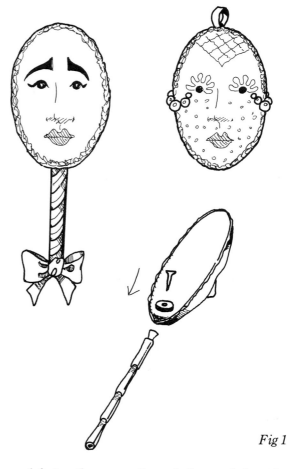

Fig 1

and fasten the screw through the mask into the handle (see Fig 1). (During this operation protect the hand with a strong glove.) The mask should support itself without flopping backwards or forwards.

4 Coat the mask with varnish front and back to seal it.

To finish

1 Mark the eye positions with pencil and make holes with a bradawl.
2 To finish the surface of the mask. Fill any hollows with plastic filler and sand down until smooth.

For the white mask

1 Make a covering base by mixing the plaster with the white paint and stirring well. This is similar to the old method of making 'gesso'. Give the mask 2 or 3 coats allowing time to dry in between. The finish is rather like that of a whitened ceiling to a room.
2 If you feel confident the features may be painted straight onto the face. Otherwise make preliminary drawings in pencil which can be rubbed off.
3 Cover the handle with ribbon (see below).
4 Glue the silver braid round the edge of the mask.

For the gold mask
1 Follow Method up to varnishing stage.
2 Cover varnished face with gold paint.
3 Decorate with patterns of sequins and beads. Make small holes at the sides and thread loops of small pearls or shells into them securing the ends with glue on the reverse of the mask.
4 Cover the handle with ribbon (see below).
5 Glue the gold braid in place.

To bind the cane handle with ribbon

For the white mask
1 Take 1m (1yd) of red and 50cm (½yd) of turquoise blue satin ribbon 4cm (1½in) wide.
2 Start off at the top of the handle with the red ribbon at an angle so that it winds neatly round the cane. Anchor the end with a dab of glue.
3 About halfway down glue the end of the turquoise ribbon to the cane and carry on winding the red ribbon over it. Bind the ribbon over the end of the cane

and knot the 2 ribbons together. Finish with a bow and trim the ends to points.

Alternatively, to create 'barber's pole' stripe, have the same 2 colours of ribbon in equal amounts. Start both ribbons off at the top but have one colour slightly below the other.

For the gold mask
Plain white trimming suits the elaborate mask best so bind the handle with 2 pieces of white satin ribbon and continue as above.

To line the mask
This is not necessary but a smoother finish can be created by covering the inside with paper or thin fabric.
1 Draw round the mask oval. Cut out the fabric.
2 Clip all round the edge to a depth of about 1cm (½in). Spread glue on the inside of the mask and press the lining in place.
3 Cut into the angles of the nose space, glue the flaps down inside and pierce the eyeholes again.

SUN HAT

 This delightful variation on the traditional sun hat is easy to make. It has a circular-stitched brim and a six-panelled crown, one of the panels having a pocket. Inside the pocket lives a little clown finger puppet to keep everyone amused. Even children who dislike wearing a hat will enjoy this one but be prepared to make more than one puppet as the first one may well get lost.

The material suggested, white cotton piqué, is crisp and cool but any firm white cotton fabric would be suitable. Piqué is a corded cotton so treat it as a one-way fabric. As with any pattern containing lots of curved sections joined horizontally and vertically, caution must be taken to see that every seam is identical and that the correct SA is observed so the lining will fit the crown and the crown will fit the brim exactly.

This pattern is for a 52cm (20in) head size and will fit a child of about 2 years old. Children's heads vary a great deal and it is far better to make the hat too big than too small. The pattern can also be used (minus pocket and clown) for a winter hat for a little boy or girl. Use a bright cotton corduroy or plain velvet for the outer fabric and toning silk for the lining. Make a button in the fabric and sew it to the top centre.*

 ## MATERIALS

60cm (24in) white cotton piqué 92cm (36in) wide
25cm (10in) white polycotton 114cm (45in) wide
25cm (10in) medium-weight interfacing 92cm (36in) wide
10cm (4in) bright red bias binding 1cm (½in) wide
Approx 58cm (23in) white cotton tape 2cm (¾in) wide
13×20cm (5×8in) piece of yellow and white dotted cotton fabric
1 skein of bright red tapisserie wool or 3 ply knitting wool
13cm (5in) square white felt
30cm (12in) royal blue satin ribbon 3cm (1½in) wide
Approx 3 pinches of toy filling or cotton wool
Embroidery threads in royal blue, black and red
Sewing threads in white and red

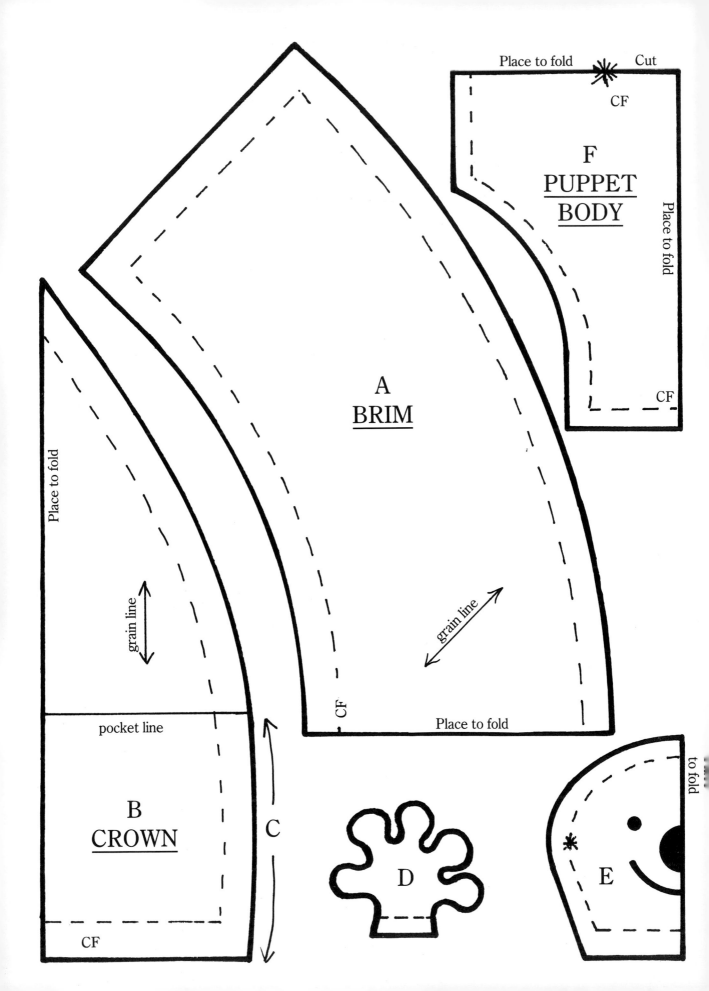

Place to fold   Cut

CF

F
**PUPPET
BODY**

Place to fold

CF

A
BRIM

grain line

CF

Place to fold

Place to fold

grain line

pocket line

C

B
CROWN

CF

D

E

to fold

METHOD

1 Make patterns (opposite).
2 Cut piece A 4 times in piqué and twice in interfacing.
3 Cut piece B 6 times in piqué and 6 times in polycotton.
4 Cut piece C once each in piqué, polycotton and interfacing.
5 Cut E twice in white felt.
6 Cut D twice in white felt and interfacing (see page 7).
7 Cut F once in dotty cotton.
(NB There is a SA of 1cm (½in) on hat pieces and ½cm (¼in) on others except D where the wrist edge only has a SA of ½cm (¼in).)
8 Transfer markings to fabrics.
9 Back the face piece with a little patch of interfacing.
10 Embroider the features (see pages 10-11).

Finger puppet

1 Place 2 head pieces RS tog and sew round leaving neck edge open.
2 Turn out the head, stuff it and close off the neck.
3 Take the body piece and cut slit at neck.
4 Fold suit in half, RS tog. Sew underarm seams but leave rest open.
5 Turn out the suit and press SA on wrist edges to the inside. Insert each hand and top-stitch across close to the edge of the sleeve.
6 Push a pinch of stuffing into each arm and top-stitch across the arm at the shoulder to enclose it.
7 Insert the head into the neck space tucking in the SA and top-stitch across close to the edge of the suit.
8 Turn up the bottom edge of the suit in a narrow hem.
9 To make the hair, pull the lengths of wool through the seamed edge of the head leaving loops of about 5cm (2in). Top-stitch round the head seam close to the edge enclosing the loop stitching (see Fig 1). Trim the hair down to 2cm (1in).
10 Make frill (see page 15).

Hat

1 Apply interfacing to back of pocket.
2 Place pocket and lining WS tog and apply red bias to the top edge.

Top-stitch across base of loops

Fig 1

3 Place the pocket on one of the crown sections and sew down each side.
4 Sew crown sections RS tog in two sets of three then both sets together. Do same with lining sections.
5 Place lining inside crown WS tog with seams matching. Sew round head seam line.
6 Apply interfacing to two of the brim sections. Place them RS tog and sew the side seams. Press the seams open. This is the underbrim.
7 Join the other two brim sections similarly. This is the upper brim.
8 Place upper brim and under brim RS tog. Sew round the outer edge.
9 Trim this seam down to ½cm (¼in). Turn the brim out and press the edge firmly.
10 Using the machine foot as a guide, stitch round the brim 1cm (½in) from the edge and so on over all the brim.
11 Place the brim over the crown, RS tog, matching side seams.
12 Ease the brim to fit the crown and sew round on the head seam line. Clip the SA at intervals.
13 Apply the white tape just inside the stitching line and overlap the ends at the back of the hat.
14 Press the tape to the inside and catch-stitch it to the lining inside.
15 Fasten the lining to the hat with a few stitches through the centre point of the crown.

BODY WARMER

This cosy little waistcoat is reversible with lively clown motifs appliquéd to the fronts. The size given will fit a child of about 6 years old but as the garment is not fitted it may be worn by a younger or older child. The seams are made onto the RS then flattened out and covered with contrasting tape. The front fastening is made by ribbon ties but a button and loop fastening could be used instead.

MATERIALS

50cm (20in) red polycotton 114cms (45in) wide

50cm (20in) dark blue polycotton 114cm (45in) wide

50cm (20in) polyester wadding 92cm (36in) wide

4m (4yd) red bias binding 2cm (¾in) wide

1m (40in) red satin ribbon 1cm (½in) wide

2 plain wooden beads 25mm (1in) diam

4 pieces of iron-on interfacing 15cm (6in) square

A piece of iron-on interfacing 30cm (12in) square

12×24cm (5×10in) yellow and white ½cm (¼in) check gingham

12×24cm (5×10in) blue and white ½cm (¼in) check gingham

Small scraps of red and blue polycotton cut from leftovers

Approx 4cm (2in) square scraps of felt in red, white, green and yellow

Embroidery thread in bright green, bright yellow, red and black

Sewing threads in red, to match bias tape, and black for outlines on appliqué

METHOD

1 Enlarge pattern pieces for front and back from grid (see page 114).
2 Cut out 1 back each in red and blue fabric.
3 Cut out 1 pair of fronts each in red and blue fabric.
4 Cut out 1 back and 1 pair of fronts in wadding.

5 Transfer markings to RS of red and blue fronts.
6 Back the area to be embroidered with interfacing.

Clown Motifs (see page 115)

1 For the clowns on the red side, cut out the appliqué pieces thus:
 2 body pieces in yellow gingham
 2 frills in plain blue
 2 faces in white felt
 2 hats in green felt
Embroidery is green for bells, red for noses, black for eyes, and yellow for front pompons, hands and feet.

2 For clowns on the blue side, cut the appliqué pieces thus:
 2 body pieces in blue gingham
 2 frills in plain red
 2 faces in white felt
 2 hats in yellow felt
Embroidery is green for bells, red for noses, black for eyes, and yellow for front pompons, hands and feet.

3 Back the clown body and frill pieces with interfacing.

4 Sew them to the appropriate fronts in this order (see page 115 for illustration): suit first, then frill, then face, then hat.

5 Embroider the hands, feet, nose, eyes, bell and pompons in satin stitch (see page 11) then press lightly.

Waistcoat

1 Sandwich the layers together for the fronts and back, thus: top fabric blue, middle wadding, bottom red. (The red layer will be referred to as WS.)
2 Tack the layers together just within the SA which is 25mm (1in).
3 Place fronts and back WS tog. Sew along side seams.
4 Trim the SA down to ½cm (¼in). Open out and press.
5 Cover the SA with red bias tape and sew evenly down each side.

To attach tie ribbons

1 Cut red ribbon into 2 equal halves.
2 Thread a bead on each piece down to halfway mark.

☆ CLOWN CLOTHING ☆

Fig 1

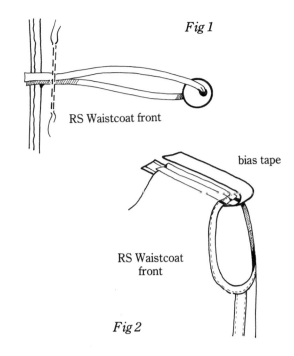

RS Waistcoat front

bias tape

RS Waistcoat front

Fig 2

3 Sew both ends of ribbon down on seam line on each front where marked (see Fig 1).

To assemble rest of waistcoat

1 Fully bind each armhole edge leaving the ends of binding tape raw (see page 9).
2 Place shoulders WS tog and sew each shoulder seam. Trim SA down and open out.
3 Cut a piece of red bias tape long enough to cover both sides of a shoulder seam in one continuous strip (see Fig 2).
4 Starting at neck edge place tape over shoulder seam then fold it inside to cover the other side of the seam and meet itself again at the neck edge. Sew down at each side.
5 Trim off excess tape at neck edge.
6 Bind round the whole of the waistcoat edge (see page 9).

Sun Hat and Body Warmer

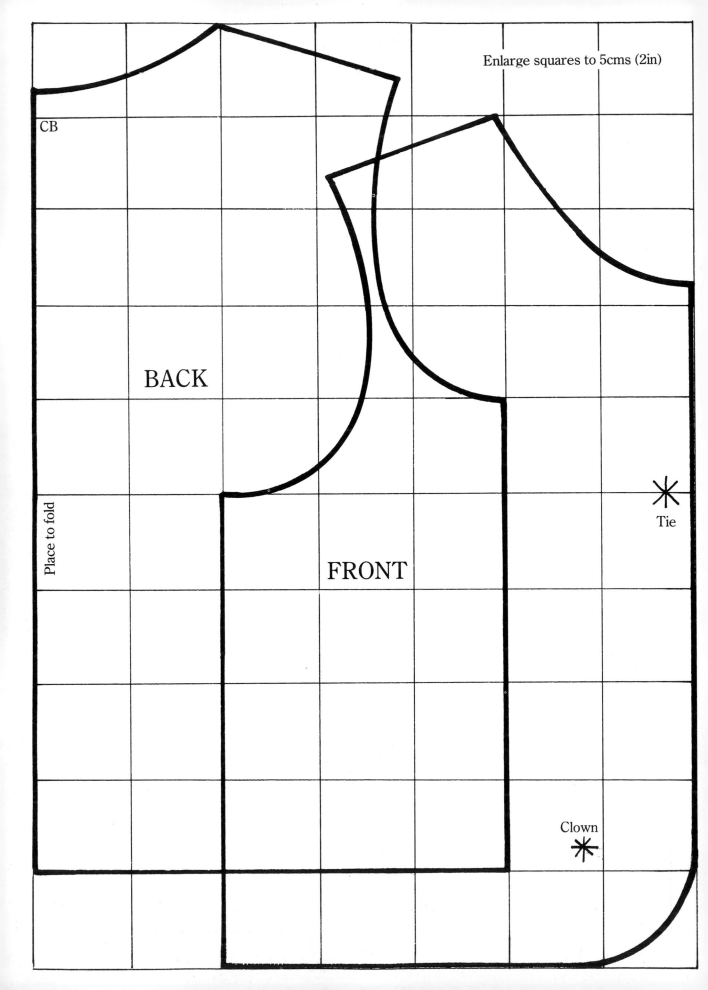

Enlarge squares to 5cms (2in)

CB

BACK

Place to fold

FRONT

✳ Tie

Clown ✳

Pattern for appliqué figure

AUGUSTE DRESSING-UP OUTFIT

Every child loves dressing up as somebody else and the clown is probably the favourite character to copy. Make the basic outfit and allow the small person to use his or her imagination to complete the costume. There are so many variations possible on this type of comical clown that they are well worth exploring. Make the baggy trousers and tail coat to start with and add other items as they become available. A pair of white gloves (miles too big) or fingerless gloves look good. The flashy coat can be worn over a string vest and the trousers held up by braces (suspenders). A trip to the nearest joke shop will furnish the clown with a water-squirting flower for the lapel and most toy shops sell face paints. If a red nose is desired it is best to make one from a soft sponge ball with a slit cut in it, rather than a hard plastic one which hurts the nose terribly after a few minutes wear. Make sure the clown's tears are not real ones!

The outfit consists of a tail coat with kimono sleeve and front Velcro (nylon tape) fastening, silver lamé lapels and tails with contrast lining; baggy tartan trousers with elastic at waist and ankles; a 'bald wig' of stockinette with appliqué eyebrows on front section and a large bow tie on elastic.

The pattern given here will fit a child of about 5 years old but as it is loose fitting it can be stretched to fit a bigger or gathered to fit a smaller child. There is no need to match up the tartan on the trousers – just get the horizontal stripes in the same position.

MATERIALS

1.50m (1½yd) bright red cotton drill or fairly heavy cotton 114cms (45in) wide

A piece of silver lamé (a fairly heavy metallic fabric) 36cm (14in) square

30cm (12in) blue silky lining fabric 114cm (45in) wide

1m (1yd) red and blue dominant tartan fabric 150cm (60in) wide (dress-weight wool or brushed cotton)

46cm (18in) flesh stockinette 50cm (20in) wide

Approx 66cm (26in) beige bias binding 1cm (½in) wide

A small piece of black felt 8cm (3in) square

50g (2oz) bright red extra thick knitting wool or rug wool cut into 36cm (14in) lengths

A piece of iron-on interfacing 46×30cm (18×12in)

A piece of yellow and white polka-dot cotton 61×20cm (24×8in)

60cm (24in) strong elastic 1cm (½in) wide (for waist)

50cm (20in) elastic ½cm (¼in) wide (for ankles)

36cm (14in) round elastic (for neck tie)

53cm (21in) round elastic (for wig)

3 flat white buttons for front trim 2cm (¾in) diam

2 very big flat buttons for back trim

2m (2yd) red bias binding 1cm (½in) wide

Machine threads in red, black, yellow and beige

3 Velcro dots or patches or 12cm (4½in) strip of Velcro

METHOD

To make the trousers

1 Cut the tartan fabric vertically into 2 equal parts to give 2 panels each 1m (1yd) long×76cm (30in) wide.

2 Fold each panel in half vertically RS tog and sew the inside leg seam up to 36cm (14in) from top edge. Finish off the seams inside if necessary.

3 Turn 1 leg RS out and place it inside the other leg matching up crotch seams. Sew round and finish off seams inside.

4 To provide a casing for the elastic, make a hem of 25mm (1in) at the bottom of each leg and one of 4cm (1½in) at the waist. Leave a small gap in each to allow the elastic through.

5 Thread the correct amount of elastic through waist and overlap the ends (see page 9). Sew across and close up the gap in the hem.

6 Thread the elastics in the ankles in the same way but use a weaver's knot (page 9) to join.

To make the coat

1 Enlarge the pattern from the grid (see page 119).

2 Transfer markings to fabrics.

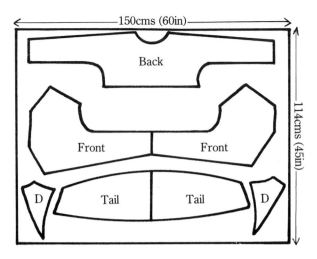

Fig 1 Layout for coat

3 Cut coat pieces from red drill as shown in layout (Fig 1).
4 Cut out 1 pair of tails from lining fabric.
5 Cut out 1 pair of lapels from interfacing and silver lamé.
(NB There is a SA of 1cm (½in) on all pieces.)

Tails
1 Place both tails RS tog and sew CB seam to mark.
2 Place tail linings RS tog and sew CB to mark.
3 Press open the seams and place lining and tails RS tog. Sew round leaving top line open.
4 Clip the corners and SA and turn out the tails through the top opening.
5 Poke out the points carefully and press.
6 Close along seam line at top.

Coat top
1 Place back and fronts RS tog. Sew underarm seams.
2 Sew shoulder seams from wrist to mark. Finish off seams inside.
3 Back the lapels with interfacing.
4 Place lapels and silver lapels RS tog. Sew round outer edge seam leaving chest edge and shoulder edge open.
5 Clip the corners and turn out. Press lightly on reverse then treat as one layer.
6 Place lapels right way up on fronts of coat and sew along chest seam.
7 Turn the coat inside out and complete each shoulder seam enclosing the edge of the lapel in the seam.
8 Place tail section RS tog with coat top at waistline matching CB seam to CB of coat. Sew across.
9 Apply one edge of bias tape to RS of edge of coat all round including inside back where tails join. Start with the tape at CB.

10 Trim all the SA to ½cm (¼in).
11 Turn the binding onto the inside and sew all round.
12 Make hems at sleeve ends.
13 Sew 2 large buttons at the back waist level.
14 Sew Velcro fastenings on fronts to overlap one side or the other.
15 Sew 3 smaller buttons to front overlap.

Bald Wig
1 Make patterns (see pages 120-1).
2 Transfer pattern markings to fabrics.
3 Cut out pieces A, B and C once each in double stockinette.
4 Cut out F twice in black felt.
(NB There is a SA of 1cm (½in) on A, B and C, and none on F.)
5 Stay-stitch round piece A. Apply eyebrows to RS.
6 Make the darts in piece B. Taper them carefully to avoid bulk.
7 Clip inside the darts and flatten them out.
8 Stay-stitch round B.
9 Stay-stitch round C.
10 Apply the hair to RS of C along the top curve, avoiding the SA at each end (see page 14).
11 Join section C to B, RS tog.
12 Join section A to B, RS tog, matching CF and sides.
13 Apply bias tape to outer edge and turn to inside (see page 9). Leave a gap to thread elastic through.
14 Check that the wig fits the child's head, then knot the elastic and close the gap in the binding.
15 Trim the wool down to approx 13cm (5in) long. The best method is to cut whilst the wig is on the child's head.

Bow Tie
1 Make the pattern (see page 120).
2 Transfer markings to fabrics.
3 Cut out piece E twice in polka-dot cotton and once in interfacing.
4 Cut a small strip of polka-dot cotton 8cm (3in) wide ×12cm (5in) long.
5 Back one piece E with interfacing.
6 Place both pieces RS tog and sew round leaving open at place marked.
7 Clip SA, turn out through opening and press.
8 Oversew opening.
9 Make a tie loop with the strip. Fold in all the raw edges 1cm (½in) and press. Fold the strip in half lengthways and press again. Pinch it round the middle of the bow and oversew the strip at the back.
10 Cut the elastic to fit the child's neck and thread this through the back of the tie loop. Join the ends with a weaver's knot (see page 9) which can be hidden inside the loop.

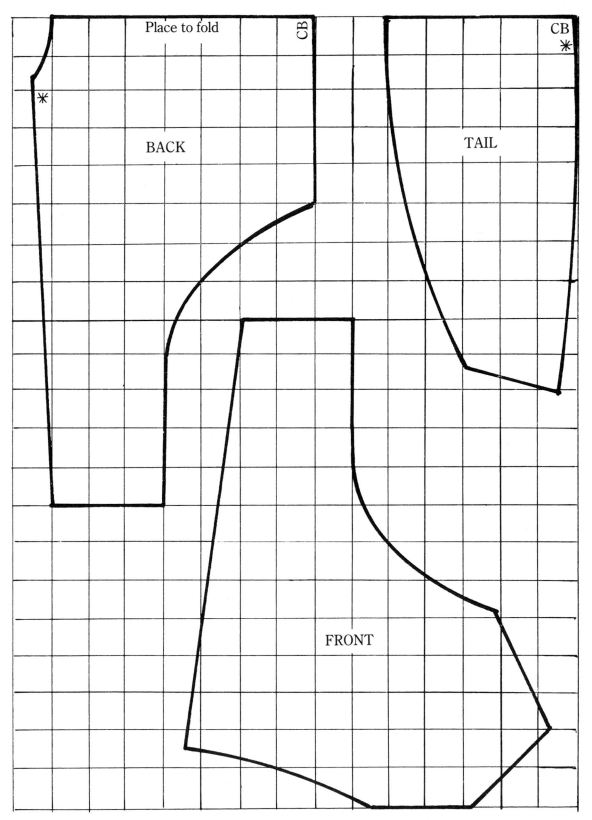

Tail coat: enlarge squares to 5cm (2in)

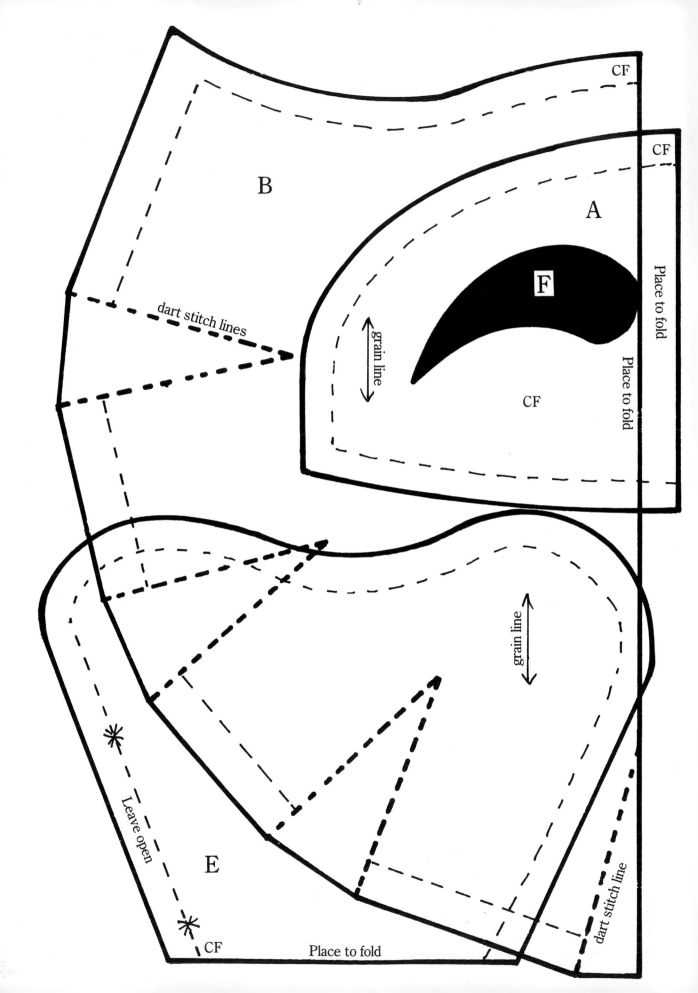

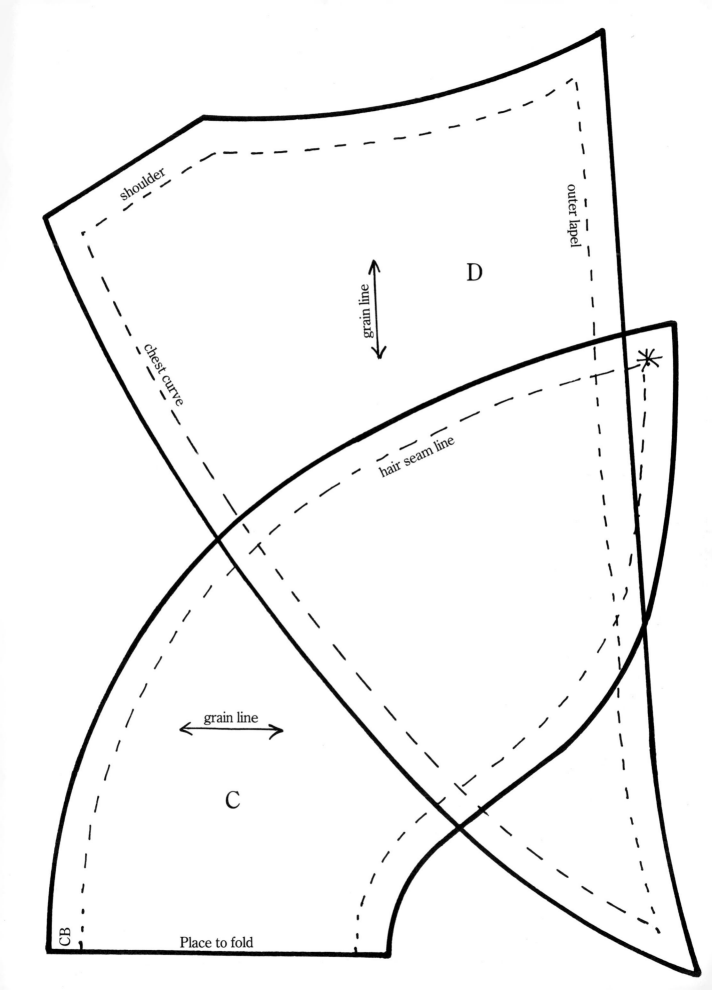

BAGGY  CLOWNS

APPLIQUÉ SHOE BAG

Besides being a shoe bag this little draw-string bag can be used in the nursery as a container for odds and ends, pencils, crayons, chalks etc, or, hanging on the wall, it makes a colourful hold-all for kitchen equip-ment. Choose the brightest fabrics for the most effect, and instead of the drawstring sew the cord from one side to the other at the top edge of the bag.

MATERIALS

2 pieces of blue cotton drill or heavy cotton 32cm (12½in) wide × 44cm (17½in) long
A piece of yellow felt 10cm (4in) deep × 13cm (5in) wide (for the name area)
A piece of red felt 13cm (5in) deep × 15cm (6in) wide (for the frame round name)
A piece of orange felt 13cm (5in) square
A piece of interfacing 15×40cm (6×16in)
Approx 20cm (8in) square scrap of orange and white tiny dotted cotton print (enough for the appliqué parts)
75cm (30in) of yellow ribbon ½cm (¼in) wide
1m (1yd) white cotton cord
50g (2oz) red DK cotton
Embroidery thread in orange, white and black
Sewing threads in blue and black

METHOD

1 Trace the appliqué sections (opposite) onto the fabrics. You will need: 2 suit bodies in polka-dot cotton, 2 arm shapes in same, 2 neck frill shapes in orange felt, 2 pairs of feet in orange felt.
2 Back the suit body fabric with interfacing before sewing down.
3 Embroider the name required on the yellow piece of felt.
4 Sew the pieces down to the bag front in this order: Red felt patch 15cms (6in) up from the base line at CF.

Yellow felt name patch leaving an even border of red showing.
The clown's neck frills.
The feet.
The suit bodies. Outline the right arm position.
The left arms.
Fill in the rest of the shapes with satin stitch, using orange thread for the hats and wrist frills, white for the hands and faces and black for the hair. Outline these areas and the eyes in back stitch using black thread.
5 The fringe is attached to the bag edge by a series of ribbon loops set in the bottom seam. Cut the yellow ribbon into 8 equal pieces and sew these in a line to the base seam line of the bag front (see Fig 1).

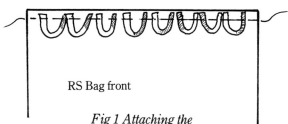

RS Bag front

Fig 1 Attaching the fringe

To make up the bag
1 Place bag front to bag back, RS tog.
2 Sew round sides and base leaving gaps at placket position in side seams 6cm (2½in) down from top edge. Make the gaps wide enough to thread the cord which means the lower placket line must be 25mm (1in) below the top one.
3 Press open the SA and sew round the placket openings.
4 Make a narrow turning along the top edge of the bag.
5 Fold the edge inside to cover the lower placket line and sew down.
6 Thread cord through (see page 9). (If the other type of handle is made omit placket spaces and attach the cord with strong stitches to top of bag at each side. Knot each cord end to stop it pulling through).

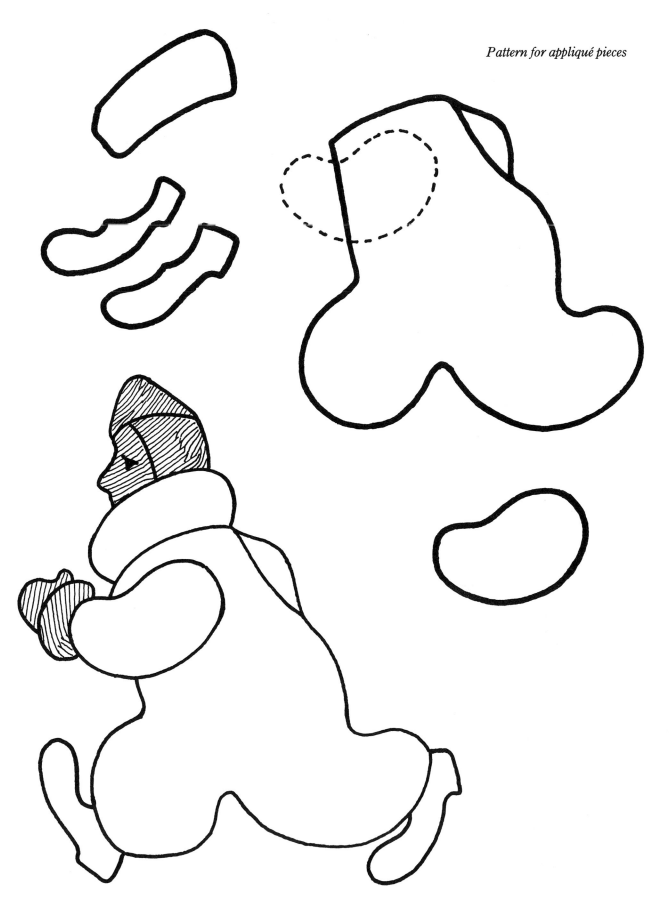

1m (1yd) of same yarn through needle

Fig 2

Fig 3

Wind tight

Trim off evenly

To complete the fringe

1 Make 8 tassels (see page 14 and Fig 2). Lengths of cotton should be 15cm (6in) with about 20 lengths to each tassel.

2 Attach 1 tassel to each ribbon loop along base of bag (Fig 3).

3 Trim the tassels off level to 10cm (4in).

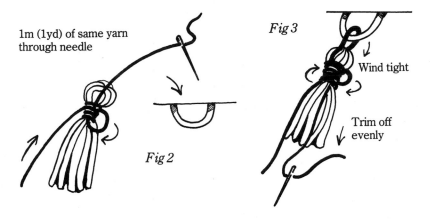

MACHINE OR HAND ⭐ ⭐

VELVET EVENING BAG

This little dolly bag could be made in a variety of fabrics to suit different occasions. Make one in light coloured satin or taffetta to match a bridesmaid's dress, or, as the sample, in black velveteen. Velveteen has a shorter, closer pile than velvet and so is easier to work with than shiny dress velvet. The bag can be as simple or elaborate as required with the addition of beads or sequins for trimming.

MATERIALS

32cm (12½in) of black velveteen 92cm (36in) wide

20cm (8in) of black lining silk 92cm (36in) wide

23cm (9in) of polyester wadding 92cm (36in) wide

23cm (9in) of muslin 92cm (36in) wide

A piece of cream-coloured spotted nylon net 25cm (10in) square

A piece of pale pink stiff net 25cm (10in) square

Pieces of black satin and cream satin 8cm (3in) square (wide satin ribbons cut up)

61cm (24in) black bias tape 2cm (¾in) wide

2 pieces of iron-on interfacing approx 10cm (4in) square

2m (2yd) of narrow silk cord in black

Black sewing thread

Pink and black embroidery thread

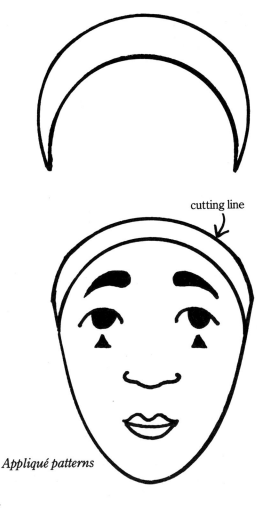

cutting line

Appliqué patterns

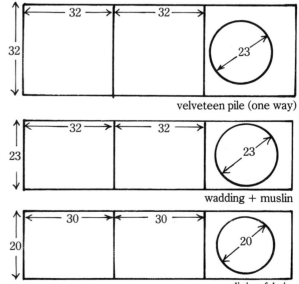

METHOD

Cutting out (see layout, Fig 1)

1 Cut 1 circle each from velveteen, wadding and muslin, 23cm (9in) diam.

2 Cut a circle of lining fabric, 20cm (8in) diam.

3 Cut front bag and back bag in velveteen, each piece 32cm (12½in) square. (Remember when making up that this is a one-way fabric.)

4 Cut 2 pieces each of muslin and wadding 23cm (9in) long×32cm (12½in) wide.

5 Cut 2 pieces of lining fabric each 20cm (8in) long×30cm (11½in) wide.

There is a SA of 1cm (½in) on linings, 25mm (1in) on wadded parts of the bag.

Appliqué decoration

This is added to the front piece before the bag is made up.

1 Trace off and cut out appliqué parts (opposite), cut face in cream satin, hat in black satin and cut a

Appliqué Shoe Bag and Velvet Evening Bag

velveteen pile (one way)

wadding + muslin

lining fabric

Fig 1 Cutting layouts (figures in centimetres)

circle of pink and one of spotted net, each 25cm (10in) diam.

2 Make puff frills (see page 15).

3 Back satin with interfacing and embroider features on face in black in back stitch using 2 strands of thread. Embroider mouth in pink satin stitch (see page 11).

4 Sew down the hat section onto the face and mount the face onto a scrap of wadding to pad it a little. Trim away excess wadding and place the motif over the gathers of the puff frills (the pink frill lies underneath the cream frill).

5 Place a piece of interfacing on the reverse of the bag front where the motif is to go.

6 Stitch the motif to the bag front through the outline of the face leaving the edge of the frills loose.

Bag

1 Make a sandwich of the fabrics, velveteen on top, wadding in the middle, then the muslin. The top fabric only extends beyond the placket line.

2 Tack round the pieces within the SA.

3 Place front and back bag RS tog and sew the side seams leaving a gap of 2cm (¾in) in each side 10cm (4in) down from the top edge.

4 Press open the SA and sew round the placket openings.

5 Place bag and base RS tog. Pin and tack round.

6 Sew round on seam line keeping circle shape smooth.

7 Trim down SA to 1cm (½in). Turn out bag.

Lining

1 Sew bag linings RS tog.

2 Sew base lining to bag lining RS tog.

3 Slip the lining inside the bag matching side seams.

Finishing off

1 Apply the black bias tape to the top edge of the bag.

2 Fold the top edge of the bag down inside until it meets and overlaps the edge of the wadding and lining with the bias tape forming the placket.

3 Tack, then sew the placket lines.

4 Thread the cords through the placket space.

5 Tie the ends together with weaver's knots (see page 9).

INDEX

Numbers in *italics* indicate illustrations.